Also by Evan Morris

Making Whoopee: Words of Love for Lovers of Words
The Word Detective: Solving the Mysteries Behind Those Pesky
Words and Phrases
The Book Lover's Guide to the Internet

From
Altoids
to
Zima

The Surprising Stories
Behind 125 Brand Names

Evan Morris

A Fireside Book
Published by Simon & Schuster
New York   London   Toronto   Sydney

FIRESIDE
Rockefeller Center
1230 Avenue of the Americas
New York, NY 10020

For information regarding special discounts for bulk purchases,
please contact Simon & Schuster Special Sales at 1-800-456-6798
or business@simonandschuster.com

Manufactured in the United States of America

10   9   8   7   6   5   4   3   2

Library of Congress Cataloging-in-Publication Data
Morris, Evan.
    From Altoids to Zima : the surprising stories behind
        125 brand names / Evan Morris.
    p.   cm.
    "A Fireside book."
    Includes bibliographical references.
    1. Brand name products. I. Title.
HD69.B7M667   2004
658.8'27—dc22   2004052597

ISBN 0-7432-5797-9

To my son, Aaron Michael, with love and pride

Contents

Introduction

What's in a name? That which we call a rose
By any other name would smell as sweet.
—WILLIAM SHAKESPEARE, *Romeo and Juliet*

Welcome to a typical morning in twenty-first century America:

7:00 a.m. Your clock radio blasts you awake, terminating your recurring MasterCard nightmare with a Money Store spiel pushing second mortgages. Your eyes, still blurred from sleep, can barely make out the Sony logo on the radio as you fumble for the off switch, but you dutifully launch yourself from bed and stagger toward the kitchen. You dump a few measures of Starbucks and some water from the Brita into your Krups machine, punch the button, and head for the shower. Midway between the L'Oréal shampoo and the Pantene conditioner, you remember that today is the day the jeweler promised your Rolex would be fixed, good news, since the cheap Timex you've been wearing in the interim loses five minutes a day. Even better, you remember that today is Casual Friday at the office, so once out of the shower, your mouth still tingling from the Scope mouthwash, you bypass the ranks of Brooks Brothers and Armani in your closet and opt for Dockers, your favorite Nikes, and a Gap chambray shirt. Breakfast consists of a container of Yoplait and a Pop-Tart.

The drive to the office is uneventful except for the jerk in the Jeep who tailgates you most of the way there, giving you a tension headache that even two Advil, washed down at a stoplight with a gulp of Evian, can't seem to dent. Once you've squeezed your Miata between your boss's Lexus and a beat-up Bronco belonging to god-knows-who, your mood is not improved as you get to your office, switch on your iMac, and read your morning e-mail. Some clown on eBay has outbid you on that Pez dispenser collection in the middle of the night, and Discover Card has discovered that the Coach bag you bought for your sister's birthday has put you over your credit limit. The office manager wants to know who has been using the Xerox machine for Tupperware party invitations. And that weirdo in personnel is still trying to dragoon everyone into attending Dianetics workshops. You wonder whether Yahoo could help you find a new job.

Lunch is Taco Bell at your desk while you work on the Lucent account, followed by Altoids to kill the taste. By five o'clock, you're running on Yoo-Hoo, Visine, and M&Ms, so on the way home you decide to reward yourself with a Domino's pizza and a six-pack of Heineken. Midnight finds you fast asleep in front of a commercial for Chia Pets—with one hand still buried in a bag of Cheez Doodles.

From the Reeboks we wear to the Volkswagens we drive, the daily lives of Americans are increasingly dominated by the manufacturers' trademarks that adorn nearly everything we own. We choose our food, our clothes, our cars, our household furnishings, even our cell phones, by brand name. So ardent is our devotion to brand names that corporate logos themselves have become wearable art and commodities in their own right; the streets of America are awash in consumers playing the role of walking billboards, clad from baseball cap to sneakers in product endorsements. A time traveler from 1950 visiting, say, Disney World today might conclude that he had wandered into a convention of people all supporting someone named Tommy Hilfiger for president.

But while our fondness for pursuing particular brands (and then flaunting them like trophies of the hunt) has become a pop culture phenomenon in recent years, many of these trademarks and product names pose mysteries. We gobble M&Ms all afternoon, but what in the world do the Ms stand for? Is Häagen-Dazs ice cream Scandinavian, German, or what? Was Scotch tape invented in Scotland? Was there really ever cocaine in Coca-Cola? And does Velcro actually mean anything?

Delving into the stories behind some of our most famous brand names is the mission of this book.

* * *

The desire to claim credit is a universal human trait, and the labeling of commodities to indicate their origin or maker is as old as trade itself. Even the prehistoric paintings on the walls of the Lascaux Cave in southern France were signed by the artists, and the ancient Greeks, Romans, and Egyptians all used some sort of mark on goods to indicate who had made the item. In the Europe of the Middle Ages, members of trade guilds developed seals and marks to indicate the origin and quality of their wares (the mark of London's Goldsmiths' Hall is memorialized today in the name of the greeting card company Hallmark).

The earliest form of what we now would consider a brand or trade name was simply the name of the maker, often appended to one or more words denoting the item itself, as in "Smith's Cough Syrup." Of course, while word of mouth might build business for such a simply named brand, a wily manufacturer would usually throw in a few encouraging adjectives ("Smith's Pure and Effective Cough Syrup") to attract the attention of customers.

Often, however, mere words would not suffice to sell a product, because until the early twentieth century, any merchant had to count on a high percentage of his clientele being illiterate. Thus many brands also depended on visual symbols prominently displayed on their packaging to ensure repeat sales. The striking symbol still found on every box of Arm & Hammer baking soda, for example, is a relic of the low literacy rate of the mid-nineteenth century.

While the nineteenth century was characterized by brand names tied to the personal name of the inventor or purveyor of the product, in the twentieth century the trend was more toward product names that functioned as mini-advertisements for the product itself. Usually these were combinations of existing words, albeit sometimes with novel spellings (Krispy Kreme) or in truncated, whimsical forms (Jell-O, combining a variation of *gelatin* with an enthusiastic suffix). Occasionally, manufacturers picked names whose connection to the reality of their product was not immediately evident, as in the case of Grape-Nuts, a breakfast cereal containing neither grapes nor nuts.

The twentieth century saw an explosion of brands and brand names; in fact, the vast majority of brand names have appeared within the past one hundred years. But as the century drew to a close, it became apparent that a major problem was facing the coiners of new brand names: they had literally begun to run out of words. The stock of useful English words not already in use in brand names (and thus protected by trademark laws) was dwindling, and picking a name even vaguely similar to an existing brand was courting costly litigation.

Thus began the age of synthetic brand names. There have always been some made-up brand names, Kodak being a notable example. But the late twentieth century saw the transformation of the entire process of naming, from picking a word or two to slap on your product to creating entirely new words, quasi words that had never existed before, for your label. And as any market abhors a vacuum, the same period produced a flood of naming consultants and firms who would, for fees ranging from thousands to millions of dollars, switch on their thinking caps and produce a Brave New Name never before heard on earth but sure to be on every consumer's lips by the holiday shopping season. At least that was how it was supposed to work.

One of the earliest, and still perhaps the most famous, synthetic namings took place in 1972, when Esso spent three years and in the neighborhood of $100 million of its stockholders' money to change its name, under the guidance of naming consultants of course, to Exxon. The new name was not a big hit with pundits, but the buying public didn't seem to mind those two *x*'s in the middle and the fact that Exxon meant absolutely nothing, so the floodgates of language opened to admit a tsunami of similar nonsense-names in the ensuing decades.

Today devising new brand names is big business, with the average new name running from $40,000 to christen a mom-and-pop operation to millions of dollars to divine a moniker for a fiber-optic network. For their money, customers of naming firms typically get surveys and focus groups of the breadth (and cost) normally associated with national political campaigns, as well as a staff of in-house linguists who analyze every potential name for the implications and overtones of each consonant and vowel. Great care is taken with the sound of the new name, and letters are ranked like star athletes. Letters such as *V* and *S* are considered good, as they suggest speed, although not as strongly as *Z* (as in Zantac and Prozac). The letter *L* suggests luxury, as does *S* (think Lexus). Often bits of real words are incorporated into the new name to "suggest" an idea or virtue, as in Accenture (the new name for the former Arthur Andersen Consulting), which is said to suggest an "accent on the future" (as opposed to wallowing in Arthur Andersen's spotty past, one presumes).

The criteria for a successful name generally accepted in the naming industry are sixfold:

It must be simple.
It must be easy to remember.
It must be impossible to mispronounce.
It must not infringe on an existing trademark.
It must not have any negative connotations in English.
It must not mean anything nasty in another language.

If the end result of this process is unrecognizable as anything resembling a meaningful word, we have a winner. And bonus points are awarded if the average literate adult can't guess from the name what the actual product might be. A meaningless name, cobbled together from powerful consonants and sexy vowels with hints of wealth, white teeth, and low taxes, is the modern marketing ideal, a blank canvas onto which can be projected any product that can be bought.

And that, dear children, is why the phone company is called Verizon and Daddy washes down his Ativan with Zima.

But at the risk of endangering a multibillion-dollar industry employing liberal arts majors who might otherwise starve, a reasonable person has to wonder what naming companies do that could not be accomplished with a Scrabble set and a bottle of old-fashioned gin.

Apparently even some people in the advertising industry have been wondering the same thing. In 2003, The Design

Conspiracy, a London ad agency, set up a spoof Web site called What Brand Are You? After visitors to the site chose a "Core Value" and a "Main Goal," a computer script spat out a meaningless "personal brand name" bearing an uncanny resemblance to the product of a big-bucks naming company search project.

If there was ever any doubt that this parody was right on target, it was dispelled when its creators discovered that at least twenty of its gobbledygook creations, including such nuggets as Bivium, Libero, and Ualeo, had subsequently been registered as trademarks by visitors to the site. Of course, no one can really blame those folks for snatching up the freebies. A penny saved, after all, is a penny that can be poured into marketing whatever a Ualeo turns out to be.

There are indications, meanwhile, that the synthetic naming industry may be nearing its own Waterloo, just as "real word" naming did. Pharmaceutical naming, one of the most lucrative fields, with thousands of new products introduced every year, has recently come under scrutiny by the U.S. Food and Drug Administration. Drug names are becoming confusingly similar, raising the danger of patients receiving the wrong medication, possibly with fatal consequences. The painkiller Celebrex, for instance, sounds very similar to the antidepressant Celexa, and either of them might be mistaken for Cerebyx, an anticonvulsive drug. The FDA reportedly now rejects one third of all proposed new drug names because of their similarity to names of existing medications.

A similar level of confusion may soon lead flustered consumers who find that they can't remember the difference between Avaya and Aviva to throw in the towel and not buy either of them. This "I give up" syndrome, writ large, will pose a curious challenge to the naming industry: where do you go when you run out of non-words?

Perhaps back to real words, perhaps of another language. The new frontier of inventing brand names may be to fiddle with French, or scramble Spanish, or invoke Italian, or even gamble with German.

Or, given the centrality of the graphic arts and animation to American culture today, perhaps we should simply go back to using distinctive visual symbols to denote all our brands, from pet food to popcorn to perfume. Eau de Bart Simpson, anyone?

FOOD AND DRINK

A.1. Steak Sauce

Henderson William Brand had a tough audience. As chef to England's King George IV in 1824, Brand was constantly striving to please the royal palate with new concoctions, and one day he served the king a new sauce he had developed for use on steak. The king was so pleased with Brand's invention that he bestowed the accolade "A1," meaning "the very best," on the sauce. When Brand left the king's service a few years later, he took both the recipe for the sauce and the king's name for it with him and began to market the sauce and other recipes as Brand & Co.

Unfortunately, Brand proved a better cook than a businessman, and Brand & Co. went bankrupt, leaving Brand no recourse but to sell the business to his friend W. H. Withall. In 1862, Withall entered the sauce in the International Exposition in London, where it again earned the rating of A1.

Within a few years Withall had sold Brand & Co. to another company, precipitating an eight-year legal battle with a very annoyed Brand, but by the late 1800s the dust had settled and A.1. Steak Sauce was on its way to becoming the most popular meat sauce in both Britain and North America. Now owned by Intercorp Excelle Inc., A.1. is touted as being excellent on fish, poultry, and vegetables as well as steak, but the recipe remains a closely guarded secret (although the company will admit to the "core ingredients" of both the Original and Zesty varieties as being malt vinegar, dates, mango chutney, apples, and orange marmalade).

Absolut

You've got to hand it to the Swedes. Somehow they managed to develop a new kind of premium vodka (a drink until then generally associated with its Russian homeland), package the stuff in a dorky transparent bottle that initially reminded a lot of people of urine samples, and grab a large chunk of the world vodka market, all under the guidance of a state-run liquor monopoly that officially frowns on drinking alcohol.

What made the difference for Absolut (short for Absolut Rent Brännvin, Swedish for "Absolute Pure Vodka") was one of the most brilliant advertising campaigns in history. Rather than relying on celebrity endorsements or cute animals, for more than twenty years since the product's American debut in 1979, Absolut ads have focused on the bottle or, more often, the shape of the bottle appearing in unlikely places. With captions like "Absolut Perfection" (showing the bottle with a halo), "Absolut New York" (the bottle outline superimposed on Central Park), "Absolut Adrenaline" (a bottle-shaped ski slope), "Absolut Borealis" (Aurora Borealis evoking an iridescent bottle), "Absolut D.C." (a bottle wrapped in red tape), and "Absolut Karloff" (a bottle wrapped like a mummy), Absolut ads have tweaked the public's imagination and projected a sophistication and subtlety rarely found in modern advertising, let alone liquor ads. A stunning archive of Absolut ads can be found at www.absolutad.com.

Alpo

No, it's not dog food promising to turn your dog into a mountaineer, nor does the name come from the excited noise Rover makes when he spots you with a can opener.

Alpo was one of the first canned dog foods marketed in the United States, in 1937, and was originally called All-Pro, probably meaning "all protein."

Unfortunately, there were, as the lawyers say, trademark issues, and in 1944 All-Pro was forced to change its name. But it didn't go very far, dropping only one *l* and the *r* to create the euphonious but meaningless Alpo.

Altoids

These "Curiously Strong" peppermint lozenges in the metal boxes were introduced in nineteenth-century London not as breath fresheners but as a remedy for indigestion. One 1920s advertisement run by the manufacturer, Smith & Company, made it clear that anyone venturing down to dinner without Altoids at the ready was courting gastric disaster: "Altoids act as an antidote to poisons in the stomach. One or two taken after meals will stop any poisonous fermentation." Later ads drove home the point with jokes about the dismal indigestibility of British food.

Altoids were originally marketed through pharmacies, and to pump up the medicinal angle, Smith & Co. tacked the scientific-sounding -*oid* suffix (from the Greek, meaning "in the form of") onto their product. (Apparently quite taken with the idea, Smith also at the time marketed remedies called Benoids, Zenoids, Cyphoids, and Notoids.)

The "Alt" in Altoids is said by the manufacturer to derive from the Latin word for "change," but a more logical source would be the Latin *altus*, or "high," making "Altoid" equivalent to "the highest or best oid." The suffix -*oid* seems to be passé in pharmacological circles today, having been supplanted by the meaningless -*ac* of Prozac and Zantac and the -*il* of Elavil and Paxil.

Altoids are still made in Britain and were introduced in the United States in 1918, although their current popularity is due largely to the company's quirky ("Nice Altoids!") ad campaign launched in 1995. The distinctive Altoids tins, now issued as limited-series collectibles, were introduced in the 1920s. Prior to then, the mints were sold in small, presumably very fragrant, cardboard boxes.

Arm & Hammer

Without a doubt one of the most widely recognized trade symbols in the world, the muscular arm and hand holding a blacksmith's hammer within a red circle on the yellow box of Arm & Hammer baking soda has never really been fully explained.

The symbol was first used when Dr. Austin Church founded the Vulcan Spice Mill, a small store selling a variety of imported spices, in Brooklyn, New York, in the mid-nineteenth century. Vulcan, the Roman god of fire, was associated with blacksmiths, so why Church chose the name for his spice business is anyone's guess. But in an age of widespread illiteracy when visual symbols were the key to forging customer loyalty, Church chose a blacksmith's arm and hammer for his shop sign.

In 1846, sodium bicarbonate (aka baking soda) was becoming popular for cooking, and Church formed a company with John Dwight to market the new product. Over the following two decades, Church and Dwight marketed baking soda under a variety of names and distributed highly popular baking soda cookbooks via direct mail. When Austin Church retired in 1867, his two sons formed their own company, Church & Co., resurrecting their father's old "arm and hammer" logo for use on the baking soda boxes. In 1896, the Church sons merged with their father's old firm under the name Church & Dwight, and within a few years was producing baking soda using the Vulcan logo and the brand name Arm & Hammer.

Today, Arm & Hammer baking soda is found in 95 percent of all American households and still produced by Church & Dwight Co., Inc.

Bacardi

Yes, that's a bat on the label. Don Facundo Bacardi Massó was only fifteen years old when his family emigrated from Spain to Cuba in 1814. After a career in wine importation and extensive experimentation with different formulas for making rum, in 1862 Don Facundo established the Bacardi distillery in Santiago de Cuba, where he and his brothers filtered their rum through charcoal, a process Don Facundo had developed.

Don Facundo's wife, Doña Amalia Lucía Victoria Moreau, suggested that the bat would make a good symbol for the new Bacardi rum. She had noticed a colony of fruit bats living in the rafters of the distillery, and knew that in Cuban lore bats were considered harbingers of good luck and prosperity. The distinctive visual trademark of the bat, in an era of widespread illiteracy, helped to make Bacardi the most popular rum in Cuba and eventually one of the world's leading brands.

Betty Crocker

There's always been a bit less than meets the eye to Betty Crocker, the now-octogenarian with the ever-youthful face found on the General Mills baking products bearing her name. It's not just that Betty cannot possibly look that good after so many years. It's that she never existed in the first place. On the other hand, that little fact didn't stop her from once being voted the second-most famous woman in America.

Betty Crocker was born in the offices of the Washburn Crosby Company in Minneapolis in 1921. As one of the largest milling companies in the United States (later to combine with other millers into General Mills), Washburn Crosby had been receiving hundreds of questions from consumers about baking with its products. To make its replies more personal, the company invented the character Betty Crocker, combining the "warm and friendly" name Betty with the surname of a former Washburn executive, William Crocker.

For the first few years, Betty was just a signature, but in 1924 she made her radio debut in a company-sponsored cooking show. As the show was not carried on a network, Betty was actually played by a different actress in each of the thirteen cities where the show was broadcast. Eventually, the *Betty Crocker's Cooking School of the Air* became a national show and ran for twenty-four years.

In 1936, America finally got its first peek at Betty Crocker in company ads and on product packages. In an early example of morphing, an artist combined the features of all the women who worked in the company's Home Service Department to arrive at an appropriately friendly look for Betty. Betty's image changed about once every decade in the following years, and today is personified with a "multicultural" image.

Birds Eye

The logo of Birds Eye Foods, one of the world's leading makers of frozen foods, features a stylized bird with a prominent eye.

But the brand's name actually has little to do with birds. Muskrats, maybe, but not birds.

Clarence Birdseye (one word) was born in Brooklyn, New York, in 1886 and spent his summers on a Long Island farm. Clarence was a born naturalist, and at the tender age of ten he found a way to combine his love of the outdoors with a little free enterprise by trapping and selling muskrats. Young Clarence then used the proceeds of his business to buy a shotgun, presumably making the muskrats even more nervous. A few years later, at Amherst College and strapped for cash, Clarence dusted off his trapping skills and financed his education by selling rats to a Columbia University geneticist.

After a variety of jobs, many of which seemed to involve trapping small animals, Clarence found himself in Labrador and made an interesting discovery: animals frozen quickly in the deep winter tasted better than those frozen more slowly in milder weather. Although preserving food by freezing dated back to at least 1626 and the first commercial frozen food hit the market in 1875, Clarence believed that he had discovered how to make frozen food actually taste good.

Back home in the United States, Clarence experimented with flash-freezing techniques and finally succeeded in 1923, freezing rabbit and fish fillets in candy boxes using dry ice. In 1924, Clarence established the General Seafoods Company (later Birdseye Foods) to further develop his technology and market both frozen foods and freezers, and the frozen food industry was off and running.

A few years and a few mergers later, Birdseye Foods was acquired by the General Foods Corporation, who changed the name of Clarence's company to Birds Eye. Clarence himself supported the change, noting that Birds Eye was the original form of his family name. Evidently an early Birdseye ancestor had once saved the life of an English queen by shooting an attacking hawk square in the eye.

Clarence Birdseye continued to work in frozen food technology and developed inventions in many other fields (a harpoon gun, a revolutionary fishing reel, and a new papermaking process) until his death, in 1956, by which time he had amassed more than three hundred patents and an unknown number of muskrats.

Budweiser

It's always Lawyer Time in this little corner of beerland. Budweiser, the flagship beer of Anheuser-Busch and the best-selling brew in America, has been scrapping over the rights to its name for decades, and there's no sign of a letup anytime soon.

The Budweiser saga began in 1876, when the E. Anheuser Brewing Association of St. Louis, Missouri, introduced Budweiser Lager Beer. Founded in 1860 by Eberhard Anheuser, the company was renamed the Anheuser-Busch Brewing Association in 1879, recognizing the contribution and leadership of then president Adolphus Busch.

"Bud" was a hit. The decades flew by and Americans guzzled Budweiser by the barrelful (three million barrels per year by 1941, in fact). Americans continued to down Bud in massive quantities, and Budweiser became an American icon.

Meanwhile, in Czechoslovakia, trouble was brewing. It seems that when Eberhard Anheuser named his beer Budweiser, he was paying homage to the beer makers of a Czech town called Ceske Budejovice, known in Anheuser's native Germany as "Budweis." According to the folks in Budweis, their local beer has been known as Budweiser for several hundred years.

In 1895 the Czech brewery Budejovicky Pivovar (mercifully known as Budvar) began producing its own brew, marketing it under the name Budweiser Budvar, and the legal fireworks soon began.

In 1939, Anheuser-Busch and Budvar supposedly buried the trademark hatchet in the United States, giving Anheuser-Busch the American rights to the name in exchange for Budvar's ownership of the name Budweiser in much of Europe. But as Anheuser-Busch expanded into and began to dominate international markets, skirmishing flared again. The Czechs even took offense at Budweiser's slogan "The King of Beers," noting that Budweis brewers had called their product "The Beer of Kings" since the sixteenth century. And Budvar partisans pointed out that A-B's Budweiser wasn't even legally considered beer in Germany, where the *Reinheitsgebot* (Beer Purity Regulations) dating back to 1516 strictly forbid the use of rice in brewing beer.

In recent years plucky Budvar has again won the right to use the names Budweiser and Bud in the European Union countries, but court cases continue to rage from Sweden to Hong Kong. Budvar's current tactic is to sell its beer in the United States as Czechvar, hoping that word of mouth about what they call (in a whisper, of course) "the real Budweiser" will win them the fame in U.S. bars that they have lost, at least for the moment, in the U.S. courts.

Canada Dry

Dry is one of those basic English words that have been around long enough to acquire all sorts of meanings only tangentially related to their primary definition, which in the case of *dry* pretty much amounts to "not wet."

In a figurative sense, however, *dry* can mean, among other things, insensitive or unemotional, caustically witty ("dry humor"), barren or unfruitful, miserly, plain, unattractive, dull, stiff or overly formal, or, of course, very thirsty. *Dry* is even an American slang term applied to those locales that forbid the consumption or sale of alcohol.

A more pleasant sense of *dry*, dating back to at least 1700, is used among wine connoisseurs to mean "free from sweetness or fruity flavor," which in many wines is a desirable attribute.

Now, fast-forward to Canada in 1904, where Toronto pharmacist and entrepreneur John J. McLaughlin was searching for a winning soft-drink formula to add to his line of bottled soda water. Most ginger ales of the day were syrupy concoctions, dark in color and extremely sweet. McLaughlin was looking for something brighter and lighter, and after many experiments he finally perfected his dream beverage. In 1919 he began exporting it to New York City as Canada Dry Pale Ginger Ale, and within a few years established his first American factory in Manhattan. While most carbonated beverages at that time were sold through corner drugstores, McLaughlin pioneered distribution at ball games, beaches, and anywhere people gathered.

By the 1920s, Canada Dry had been acquired by P. D. Saylor and Associates and was on the verge of becoming a nationwide brand in the United States. Ironically, it was one of the other meanings of the word *dry*—prohibiting the sale of alcohol— that gave Canada Dry its biggest boost. Canada Dry Ginger Ale turned out to be just right for disguising the often raw taste of home-brewed alcohol and became the mixer of choice during Prohibition. By the 1930s, Canada Dry had added several other varieties to its line and was on its way to global success.

Chef Boyardee

Chef Boyardee? What kind of name is that? And look at the dude on the label—straight from central casting, a cheerful old guy wearing a huge chef's hat. What kind of self-respecting chef would put his name and picture on something called Beefaroni? In a can, no less. Must be an ad agency creation, phony as Betty Crocker or Charlie the Tuna.

But there really was a Chef Boyardee, and Beefaroni notwithstanding, he really was an excellent Italian chef. His name, however, was actually Hector Boiardi, and he was born in northern Italy in 1898. Hector's family immigrated to the United States when he was just seventeen, and he soon got a job alongside his older brother in the kitchen of New York's prestigious Plaza hotel. Hector, who had begun working in restaurant kitchens in Italy at the age of eleven, quickly honed his cooking skills and was a hit at the Plaza and other restaurants. In 1929, he opened his own Italian eatery, Il Giardino d'Italia, in Cleveland, where his signature spaghetti sauce became the talk of the town, with patrons asking for extra portions to take home with them. Hector began selling his spaghetti sauce, packaged with pasta and cheese for home use, and before long what had begun as a sideline became his primary occupation. To make Boiardi easier to spell for his customers, he adopted the phonetic spelling "Boyardee," and eventually sold his business to American Home Products (now International Home Foods, Inc.).

And that really is a picture of Hector on the label.

Coca-Cola

It's not surprising that Coca-Cola, probably the world's most recognized product (and certainly its most popular soft drink) has spawned a wide variety of popular stories about its origin, its effects, and the ingredients used in Coke's famous "secret formula." Most of these tales, such as the ones about Coca-Cola dissolving teeth, its supposed contraceptive powers, or the assertion that 1985s New Coke debacle was a Machiavellian gambit to divert attention from a change from the original formula, are baseless. But the most frequently heard story, that Coca-Cola originally contained cocaine, is, technically speaking, true.

Coca-Cola was invented in 1886 by John Pemberton, an Atlanta, Georgia, pharmacist. Pemberton was actually trying to

Soap Satanists to blow up Oprah on June first.

Prior to the invention of the Internet, they were known as "old wives' tales" or, to manufacturers besieged by agitated customers, simply "malicious rumors," usually easily dispelled by an official statement. But with the dawn of e-mail and the Web, stories about popular products, and their secret properties, ingredients, and scandals sometimes became a public relations nightmare for companies caught in the glare of bizarre and damaging rumors spread at the speed of light.

Like all urban legends, rumors about consumer products usually reflect deep-seated fears, particularly about the purity and safety of food, as well as paranoia about technology and, occasionally, belief in secret societies and the occult. In almost all cases, rumors about products reflect an underlying desire to return to the "good old days" before mass-produced food and high-tech gizmos, notwithstanding the fact that food contamination and unsafe products were far more prevalent before the mid-twentieth century.

Below are a few of the more notable urban legends of recent years centering on consumer products. Each of these stories has been countered with vigorous debunking efforts by the companies involved. In most cases, such efforts have slowed, but not stopped, the rumors, and they are still popping up every day in e-mail boxes all over the world.

Pop Rocks killed Mikey—Perhaps the best-known pre-Internet food rumor involves Pop Rocks, a "fizzy" candy first marketed in 1975 by General Foods. Eat Pop Rocks and drink a carbonated soda, went the tale, and your stomach will explode. In fact, the story inevitably went on, little Mikey, of LIFE cereal commercial fame, had died in just such a gruesome fashion.

This story first came to the attention of General Foods about four years after Pop Rocks were introduced, and the company mounted an all-out advertising blitz to reassure parents that their children were in no danger of exploding. It didn't work, and the "Killer Pop Rocks" story is still circulating, now through the medium of e-mail. By the way, John Gilchrist, who played Mikey in the LIFE commercials at age three, in 1971, is alive and well and working as advertising manager of a New York City radio station. And the two other kids in the commercial really were his brothers, Michael and Tommy Gilchrist.

Mountain Dew will shrink your genitals—Some urban legends, like this one, are marked by a certain warped genius. What better to strike fear in the hearts of young men than the assertion that a soft drink overwhelmingly popular with young men will shrink or otherwise impair the body parts many young men value the most? This rumor (sometimes promising reduced sperm count as well) has been floating around since the late 1990s.

Coke and aspirin will get you high—Not unless you consider a probable stomachache a high. Both this and the "secret" that Coca-Cola makes a good spermicidal douche date back to at least the 1930s. One wonders if the children born to "Coke as birth control" believers grew up being served Pepsi by bitter parents.

Dr Pepper removed the phrase "under God" from the Pledge of Allegiance printed on its promotional cans—This one contains a grain of truth. In November 2001, in the wake of the 9/11 attacks, Dr Pepper issued a promotional can with a patriotic theme. Above a graphic of the Statue of Liberty, a banner on the can read "One Nation . . . Indivisible," eliding the words "under God" found in the full pledge. Evidently many people believed that the company had omitted mention of God for fear of offending atheists. Dr Pepper pointed out that space on the can was very limited and that "under God" would not have fit any more than the remainder of the Pledge (". . . with liberty and justice for all") would.

Procter & Gamble is run by satanists—According to this rumor, which has been making the rounds since the 1980s, the CEO of P&G appeared on a popular talk show (various versions of the tale specify the Phil Donahue, Sally Jesse

Raphael, or Jenny Jones shows) and announced that he was "coming out of the closet" to announce his worship of Satan. He also supposedly revealed that most of P&G's profits go to support satanic causes. Cited as evidence is the "man in the moon" P&G symbol, which is said to contain a hidden "666," the biblical "mark of the Beast" (Satan).

Denials by P&G and all three talk show hosts over the past twenty years have slowed but not entirely stopped this story. But a possible explanation for the ruckus, interestingly enough, may lie in the series of lawsuits filed by P&G against its competitor Amway, suggesting that either Amway or its distributors have deliberately spread the rumor to damage P&G. The suit against Amway has been dismissed, but at least one lawsuit against an Amway distributor is still pending.

Tommy Hilfiger (or Liz Claiborne) declared on the *Oprah Winfrey Show* that they never intended for "blacks or Asians" to wear the clothes they design—Making the rounds since the 1990s, this one has been denied by Tommy, Liz, and Oprah but will almost certainly crop up again attributed to another designer.

Don't buy Coke after June first—Multiple variants of this story made the e-mail rounds shortly after the September 11 attacks. The basic scenario involves a person doing a small favor for someone of Middle Eastern appearance, who then rewards his benefactor with a whispered warning not to drink Coke, drink Pepsi, fly on a certain airline, or visit a certain city after a certain date, after which, it is implied, said product or venue will be the target of a terrorist attack.

Coca-Cola took the spread of this rumor seriously enough to post a statement on its Web site assuring consumers that mass poisoning of its products was impossible, but given the vulnerability felt by the public in the wake of 9/11, this rumor will probably be active for at least the next few years.

Your friend, Bill Gates—An e-mail from Microsoft's chairman asks you to forward his message to all your friends in order to test a new kind of tracking software, in return for which you will receive $1,000. This hoax first appeared in 1997 and has since mutated to offer rewards from almost every prestigious manufacturer from Adidas to Victoria's Secret. The key to its spread is widespread ignorance of Internet technology, which does not yet (and may never) allow the tracing of forwarded messages, let alone millions of them. Perhaps, if such a program is developed someday, it may stop the spread of such hoaxes.

concoct a headache remedy, but once he mixed his special syrup with carbonated water, and a few customers tasted the result, he realized that he had the makings of a popular soda fountain beverage. The name Coca-Cola was coined by Pemberton's bookkeeper, Frank Robinson, who also wrote out the new name in the expressive script that has become Coca-Cola's signature logo.

Though the Coca-Cola Company apparently would rather not talk about the origin of its name in detail, it's clear that Robinson derived "Coca-Cola" from two of the drink's ingredients: cola from the cola nut, and extract of coca leaf, also the source of cocaine. Cocaine was a common ingredient of nineteenth-century patent medicines, and by the standards of the day Coca-Cola contained a minuscule amount that probably had no effect on its consumers. Still, by the early 1890s there was a rising tide of anti-cocaine sentiment, and Atlanta businessman Asa Candler, who acquired the Coca-Cola Company in 1891, steadily decreased even the tiny amount of the drug in the recipe. There is some evidence that the only reason Candler kept putting even minute amounts of coca extract in the drink was the belief that to omit it entirely might cause Coca-Cola, by then besieged by imitators, to lose its trademark. In any event, Coca-Cola was completely cocaine free by 1929.

The name Coke appeared in popular usage as a short form of Coca-Cola just before World War I but was often applied as a generic term to any cola drink (and used by Coca-Cola's competitors, including the now long-defunct Koke Company) until 1940, when the U.S. Supreme Court ruled that the name Coke rightfully belongs to the Coca-Cola Company.

Cracker Jack

Manufacturers have an eerie fondness for hypothetically laying their products end-to-end and reporting the results. So I feel obliged to play along and tell you that if all the Cracker Jack snacks ever sold were thus deployed, the trail of peanuts and popcorn would stretch around the earth more than sixty-nine times. And presumably make a lot of squirrels very happy.

According to corporate lore, an early form of Cracker Jack was introduced in 1893 at the World's Columbian Exposition, Chicago's first world's fair, by the candy-making firm of F. W. Rueckheim and Brother. Popcorn, Cracker Jack's primary ingredient, had been invented by American Indians long ago, and some New England tribes had been known to coat their popcorn with maple syrup to preserve it. But coating the corn with molasses, as Frederick William Rueckheim had done, had produced only sticky globs until his brother, Louis, developed a secret method (still a company secret, by the way) of keeping the popcorn from sticking together. The inspired addition of peanuts made the Rueckheims' confection a crowd-pleaser. Just what they called their mixture at first is unrecorded, but in 1896 Louis gave a sample to a salesman who exclaimed, "That's crackerjack!" F.W. chimed in with "So it is."

At the time, *crackerjack* was a current popular slang adjective meaning "excellent," "exceptionally fine," or "splendid," and as a noun meant "a skillful or expert person." The root of *crackerjack* is an antiquated sense of the verb *to crack* meaning "to boast or act boldly," coupled with *jack,* the proper name used as a generic synonym for "thing or person" (the same sense underlying the automobile jack). This "boast" sense of *crack* is still heard in the sort of short, sharp comment known as a crack, as well as in the derogatory term *cracker* applied to poor southern whites, which originally derided white residents of Georgia as boastful and foolishly bold.

Rueckheim promptly ran out and trademarked Cracker Jack as well as the slogan "The more you eat, the more you want." The next few years saw Cracker Jack prosper due to several good ideas and one stroke of incredible luck. The company developed its foil-sealed boxes in 1902, and in 1912 decided to put small prizes right in the box, rather than, as other companies did, enclosing coupons that had to be redeemed by mail. But its real lucky break came in 1908 with the hit song "Take Me Out to the Ball Game," by Jack Norworth and Albert Von Tilzer (neither of whom had ever been to a baseball game at the time), which included the line "Buy me some peanuts and Cracker Jack." The song was a home run for Cracker Jack, and put the company (now owned by Frito-Lay) well on its way to girding the earth with peanuts and popcorn.

Cuervo

There's a good reason Cuervo tequila is the most popular in the world. José Cuervo is the man who invented tequila.

In 1758, Don José Antonio de Cuervo was granted a parcel of land in Mexico, then a Spanish colony, by the king of Spain. In 1781, Don José Prudencio de Cuervo, son of Don José, began production of mezcal wine made from the blue agave, a large cactus related to aloe, in the town of Tequila. In 1795, the family received official permission from Spain to produce and distribute "mezcal wine of Tequila," soon to be known simply as tequila.

Instantly popular in Mexico, Cuervo tequila was first exported to the United States in 1873 and today U.S. sales substantially outpace those in Mexico, at least in part because margaritas, made with tequila, are the most popular mixed drink in America. The Cuervo bottle, by the way, still bears the image of a crow, a symbol adopted by José Cuervo (*cuervo* means "crow" in Spanish) back in 1795 to make his brand distinctive even to illiterate customers.

Dr Pepper

"*Doctor Pepper, so misunderstood . . .*" ran the old advertising jingle for one of America's most popular soft drinks, and no wonder. The folks who make the stuff won't even reveal exactly what's in it, although they do deny the presence of either pepper or prunes.

Dr (there is no period) Pepper was invented in 1885 by a pharmacist named Charles Alderton at Morrison's Old Corner Drug Store in Waco, Texas. Alderton, who was just fooling around at the soda fountain, gave the recipe to his boss, Wade Morrison, and there seems no doubt that Morrison came up with the Dr Pepper name. But even the Dr Pepper Company doesn't know who, if anyone, "Dr Pepper" was. One popular theory traces the name to an actual Dr. Pepper, on whose daughter (presumably the original "Pepper Upper") Morrison had an ardent crush.

Incidentally, the "10-2-4" inscription on Dr Pepper cans and bottles refers to 10 a.m., 2 p.m., and 4 p.m., the times when, according to a 1920s Columbia University study, consumers might be slumping during their workday and most in need of a shot of sugar and caffeine.

Fig Newton

Didn't know it was a trademark, did you? But only the cookies made by Nabisco are, legally speaking, Fig Newtons. Everything else is just a fig bar.

One popular theory says that Fig Newtons were named after Isaac Newton, but as much as we'd all like to see a line of famous-scientist cookies (maybe Copernicus Nut Clusters or Mandelbrot Macaroons), no such luck. It turns out that the first Fig Newtons were baked by the Kennedy Biscuit Company of Massachusetts, back in 1891. The folks at Kennedy Biscuit, which later merged into what would become Nabisco, evidently had a habit of naming their confections after local towns (Beacon Hill, Shrewsbury, etc.) and institutions (e.g., Harvard). The Fig Newton thus immortalizes the lovely Boston suburb of Newton.

Godiva

When in doubt, sex it up. Chocolate in various forms had been a fixture of the European diet since it was first imported by Spain from Mexico in the sixteenth century. Consumed at first in liquid form, by the late seventeenth century chocolate was a popular flavoring for cakes and pastry, and soon Switzerland and Belgium had become the world centers of chocolate candy making.

So when Joseph Draps founded his chocolate company in Brussels in 1926, he was not exactly breaking new ground. True, Draps had perfected a method of making his rich "boutique" chocolates smoother than the competition's, and he also understood the importance of fancy packaging to a luxury brand's success. But it fell to Draps's son, who took over the business a few years later, to come up with the key to building a worldwide chocolate empire, and to do it he drew on one of Europe's most enduring folk tales.

According to legend, Lord Leofric of Coventry in eleventh-century England was never so happy as when he was levying a new and onerous tax on his subjects. Leofric's raids on the pocketbooks of the populace drew loud protest, but he remained unmoved. Finally, even his wife, Lady Godiva, felt compelled to intercede on the people's behalf, and to change his mind she offered Leofric an intriguing deal. She would ride through the streets of Coventry, wearing nothing but her long hair, if Leofric would cut taxes. Convinced she was bluffing, Leofric agreed. But true to her word, Lady Godiva then disrobed, hopped on her horse, and trotted through town. Leofric, impressed by her chutzpah, then kept his side of the deal and slashed taxes.

What Lord Leofric apparently didn't know, however, was that Lady Godiva had announced her ride in advance and requested that the villagers stay inside with their shutters closed for the duration of her excursion. Given a choice between seeing the lord's wife naked and lower taxes, they naturally chose the tax cut and thus Lady Godiva's dignity remained unsullied. (According to one version of the legend, the town butcher, a certain Tom, couldn't resist sneaking a peek, and ever since that day voyeurs have been known as Peeping Toms.)

While chocolate is noticeably absent from the story of Lady Godiva's ride, Draps recognized that the legend was known throughout Europe and North America, and the fact that the name Godiva conjured up both wealth and nudity was unlikely to hurt sales, to put it mildly. So Joseph Draps, Jr., launched Godiva Chocolatiers and began marketing luxury handmade chocolates across Europe and, eventually, in the United States. Today the distinctive Godiva gold *ballotin,* or treasure chest, is among the most widely recognized symbols of luxury in the world.

Good & Plenty

If it seems as if Good & Plenty, the licorice candy bits that make a *chucka-chucka* castanet sound when you shake the box, has been around forever, it's because it has. Good & Plenty is actually the oldest branded candy in the United States, first produced by the Quaker City Confectionary Company of Philadelphia in 1893.

Good & Plenty cemented its position in the notoriously fickle kids' candy market in 1950, when its ads introduced Choo Choo Charlie, the engineer who made his train run on Good & Plenty, complete with a theme song accompanied by the *chucka-chucka* sound of shaking candy boxes.

The name Good & Plenty itself is apparently a double entendre, signifying that the candy is good and that there is plenty of it in the box, as well as playing off the intensifying idiom "good and . . ." (as in "good and drunk"). To a child looking to get the most bang for his nickel, the name Good & Plenty was an irresistible promise.

Grape-Nuts

It's not made from grapes and it contains no nuts. So what's up with Grape-Nuts cereal? It all goes back to C. W. Post's ideas about what was wrong with the average human diet.

In 1892, Charles William Post, then only thirty-eight years old, was concerned about his health, especially his chronically upset stomach. So he checked himself into the Battle Creek Sanitarium (run by Dr. John Harvey Kellogg, of Kellogg Cereals fame), in Michigan. During his stay, Post became convinced that Kellogg's "pure food" theories were correct, and after leaving the sanitarium set up his own medical boardinghouse and farm and set about developing a line of healthy grain-based foods.

Post's first product was Postum, a wheat-based coffee substitute, followed in 1897 by Grape-Nuts, a blend of wheat and malted barley cereals, and which just happened to make use of the wheat bran removed in the manufacture of Postum. Post once explained that "grape sugar" was formed during the baking process, and the finished cereal had a "nutty" taste. Voilà (more or less), Grape Nuts. Post marketed both Postum and Grape-Nuts under the slogan "There's a Reason," and though he never specifically explained what that reason might be, he did include a copy of his healthy-eating tract, "The Road to Wellville," in each box of cereal. Post's pamphlet, not surprisingly, advised people to drink lots of Postum, fill up on Grape-Nuts, and think positive thoughts.

Though Postum has remained largely a niche product in the years since, Grape-Nuts has been a consistently strong seller in the highly competitive breakfast cereals market.

Häagen-Dazs

Sometimes all it takes is one brilliant idea. Reuben Mattus (1913–1994) was a Polish immigrant who began his career peddling his family's ices and ice cream products from a horse-drawn wagon. After more than thirty years of selling his wares on a small scale to restaurants and stores in the Bronx, Reuben noticed something about American consumers. They wanted good ice cream, but they also wanted something exotic.

So Reuben put on his thinking cap and came up with the name Häagen-Dazs for his new line of premium, high-fat ice cream. Although it sports an umlaut and sounds Scandinavian, the name Häagen-Dazs is pure nonsense—it doesn't actually mean anything in any known language. But consumers took the bait when Mattus's creation debuted in 1961, and Häagen-Dazs was an immediate hit with everyone (except dieters, of course). An ironic footnote: Hedging his bets after he sold Häagen-Dazs to Pillsbury in 1983, Reuben Mattus went on to develop and market Mattus' Lowfat Ice Cream.

Heinz 57 Varieties

Why did "57 Varieties" become the slogan of the H. J. Heinz Company? Because Henry John Heinz happened to look up from his newspaper on the train one day in 1896.

Together with L. Clarence Noble, Heinz had launched his condiment company (originally known as Heinz & Noble) in Pittsburgh, Pennsylvania, with horseradish packed in clear glass bottles (as opposed to the tinted glass favored by competitors) so that consumers could see the purity of the product for themselves. Within a few years the company had added pickles, sauerkraut, and vinegar to its line, but the banking crisis of 1875 pushed the small company into bankruptcy.

Starting over later that same year, Heinz added ketchup— then considered an exotic new concoction—to his product line, followed shortly thereafter by red and green pepper sauce, chili sauce, mincemeat, apple butter, mustard, tomato soup, olives, pickled onions, pickled cauliflower, baked beans, and sweet pickles. By 1896 the H. J. Heinz Company was marketing dozens of products and beginning distribution of its line in Europe.

Then, one day when Heinz was riding the elevated train in New York City, an advertisement in the train car caught his eye. It was for a shoe manufacturer, boasting of "21 Styles of Shoes." The idea of using a number as a hook for advertising struck Heinz as a great idea, and after mulling it over for a few days, he decided to go with the number 57, which he had always felt was his personal lucky number. Within a week, the new Heinz slogan "57 Varieties" was appearing on billboards and in print advertisements all over the United States.

What made Heinz's choice of a slogan slightly strange was that his company was already producing sixty varieties of products and adding more every year. But Heinz was adamant in his devotion to "57 Varieties," and the slogan has been featured on Heinz products, which now number more than five thousand, ever since.

Jell-O

On March 17, 1993, according to the Jell-O Museum Web page (www.jellomuseum.com), technicians at St. Jerome Hospital in Batavia, New York, apparently having nothing better to do, hooked an electroencephalograph up to a bowl of lime Jell-O. They were amazed, the story goes, to discover that America's favorite gelatin dessert exhibits brain waves "identical" to an adult human being. Unrecorded but obviously relevant is whether the adult human used for comparison happened to work as a technician at St. Jerome Hospital.

But while lime Jell-O seems an unlikely candidate for the Nobel Prize in much of anything, it does hold the distinction of being a big hit in Salt Lake City, which consumes more of the green jiggly stuff than any other American metropolis.

For a brand name that today is recognized by 95 percent of Americans and found in 66 percent of their homes, Jell-O got off to a rocky start. The first person to patent a gelatin dessert, in 1845, was Peter Cooper, the inventor, manufacturer, and philanthropist best known for pioneering the railroad locomotive in America. But making Cooper's gelatin took the better part of a day and the product was not very popular.

A scant fifty years later, however, carpenter and cough medicine purveyor Pearle B. Wait and his wife, May Davis Wait, of LeRoy, New York, fiddled a bit with Cooper's gelatin, and by 1897 had developed easier-to-make strawberry, raspberry, orange, and lemon flavors. A name was needed for the product, and May came through with a winner—Jell-O.

Given the spelling "Jell-O," May Wait was probably thinking of *jelly*, not *gelatin*, when she dreamed up the name, but the two words share a common root. The Latin *gelare* means "to freeze," and as it percolated into various later European languages took on the connotation "to congeal" (in fact, *congeal* itself is a descendant of *gelare*). Both *gelatin* and *jelly* were originally applied to a substance produced by boiling animal bones, skins, etc., to release collagen, which jells into a semisolid as it cools. (Fruit jelly, which does not come from animals, jells because of the pectin in the fruit itself.) Today's gel-atin, including that found in Jell-O, comes from the same animal sources but is so rigorously purified that many vege-tarians consider Jell-O perfectly acceptable.

In subsequent years the Jell-O brand changed hands several times and today is owned by Kraft Foods Inc., which markets more than 150 products under the Jell-O name, including puddings, pie fillings, and Jello-O Pudding Pops. And in Jan-uary 2001, all that lime finally kicked in and Jell-O was de-clared the "Official State Snack" of Utah. EEG testing of the Utah legislature might be interesting.

KFC

Some people might call Harland Sanders a late bloomer, but by the time he put Kentucky Fried Chicken on America's tables he had already had at least a dozen careers.

Born in 1890, Sanders learned to cook at age seven after his father died and his mother was forced to go to work. At age ten, young Harland got his first real job, on a nearby farm, and by fifteen he was working as a streetcar conductor. At sixteen, he joined the Army and ended up serving in Cuba.

In the following decades, Sanders worked as a railroad fire-man, became a lawyer and practiced law, operated a steamboat on the Ohio River, sold insurance, and, in 1930, finally settled down to run a service station in Corbin, Kentucky. Just running a service station was, of course, not enough for the energetic Sanders, and soon he was putting his cooking skills to use again, providing meals for travelers, first in his own dining room and eventually in a restaurant across the road. Over the next few years he concentrated on perfecting his special recipe for fried chicken, devising the "eleven herbs and spices" of the "secret recipe" still zealously guarded by KFC. Sanders's chicken became so popular that in 1935 he was made a Kentucky Colonel in recognition of his contribution to the state's cuisine.

In 1950, however, a new highway bypassing the town of Corbin effectively put Sanders out of business, and his sole income became his $105 per month Social Security checks. Undaunted, two years later, at age sixty-two, Sanders hit the road with a plan to franchise his fried chicken, for a nickel for each chicken sold, to restaurants across the United States. Amazingly, the plan worked, and by 1964 the Colonel's chicken was being sold in more than six hundred restaurants. At age seventy-four, Sanders sold his business for $2 million and became the official spokesman for Kentucky Fried Chicken. By 1974, he was ranked as the second-most recognized celebrity in the world. Colonel Sanders died in 1980 at the age of ninety from leukemia, but his smiling image still graces KFC's packaging.

The decision to change the name of the restaurant chain from Kentucky Fried Chicken to KFC in 1991 spawned a range of bizarre rumors and urban legends, including speculation that KFC was raising vast herds of mutant Frankenchickens in secret and that the USDA had forbidden KFC to use the word *chicken* in reference to the creatures. The truth was simply that the corporation was planning to begin offering non-chicken menu items, and also thought it wise to downplay the word *fried* in an increasingly health-conscious marketplace.

Kool-Aid

There seems to be some dispute as to whether Edwin Perkins was twelve or fourteen years old when he had his idea, but it was a doozy.

Young Edward had sent away for a mail-order "start your own business" kit, and quickly set about inventing a variety of flavorings and perfumes in his mother's kitchen. Unlike many youthful experimenters, Perkins kept at it, year after year, and by 1914, at age twenty-four, he was operating his own mail-order business, selling a concentrated soft drink syrup he called Fruit Smack. But the Fruit Smack bottles were expensive to mail and often arrived damaged, so Perkins decided that product modifications were called for.

The solution, as it happened, was as close as his father's general store, where sales of the new Jell-O powdered dessert mix were booming. Perkins stopped selling the liquid Fruit Smack and began selling a concentrated drink-mix powder, which he at first called Kool-Ade, modeling the name on *lemonade*. But to Perkins, the *-ade* suffix had medicinal overtones, so he changed the name to Kool-Aid, which conveniently carried a connotation of "aiding" drinkers in remaining cool. The original flavors of Kool-Aid were cherry, lemon-lime, grape, orange, root beer, strawberry, and raspberry. Today more than 563 million gallons of Kool-Aid are consumed every year.

Krispy Kreme

The moral of this story is: ask now, or forever be puzzled.

Once upon a time (1933, to be precise), a man by the name of Ishmael Armstrong bought a doughnut shop from a New Orleans chef named Joe Lebeau. More important than the shop itself, however, was the secret recipe for raised doughnuts that came with it. By all accounts it was a miraculous recipe that produced doughnuts of unparalleled lightness and flavor, doughnuts so extraordinary that the name he had dreamed up for his confections, Krispy Kreme, had become a local legend.

Ishmael Armstrong passed the recipe down to his nephew Plumie Rudolph, whose son Vernon opened a wholesale doughnut business in Winston-Salem, North Carolina, in 1937. Krispy Kreme at first sold its doughnuts only to grocery stores, but so many people stopped by the factory asking to buy fresh doughnuts that Vernon Rudolph finally cut a take-out window in the building's wall and began selling directly to customers.

By the time of Rudolph's death in 1973, Krispy Kreme was a booming franchise operation with thousands of dedicated customers, but the company's acquisition shortly thereafter by Beatrice Foods is now considered the low point of Krispy Kreme history. To cut costs, Beatrice changed the famous secret recipe, alienating customers and infuriating franchise operators. Not surprisingly, when Beatrice decided to sell the company in 1981, Krispy Kreme franchise owners banded together to buy back their beloved company and immediately restored the original recipe to its place of honor.

With more than three hundred stores in the United States and Canada, Krispy Kreme is now an American icon, and only one nagging question remains: what's with the name Krispy Kreme? The company's signature raised doughnuts aren't exactly crispy, and contain no creme filling. It's a question that, unfortunately, is destined to forever remain a mystery. It seems that when Ishmael Armstrong bought Joe Lebeau's doughnut shop and recipe back in 1933, he simply forgot to ask about the origin of the name. And since Mr. Lebeau has long since shuffled off to that great doughnut shop in the sky, the best we can do is ponder the possibilities while we munch our doughnuts.

Life Savers

Ever wonder how Life Savers candy is made? Don't deny it, we all have. How do they get them all the same size? How do they put the little hole in the middle? And, of course, what happened to the candy that was where the hole is before they made the hole?

The answer turns out to depend on what kind of Life Savers you mean. Mints (Pep-O-Mint, Wintergreen, etc.) are made from a paste of sugar, corn syrup, and mint oils pressed into tiny doughnut-shaped molds. Drops (fruit flavors, etc.) are a bit trickier. The flavoring is mixed into corn syrup, into which a rod is then dipped, forming a "rope" of candy. The hole is actually the space taken up by the rod in the center of the "rope," which is then cut from each side to make the final candies. So in neither case is there ever any missing candy from the hole.

When Good Brands Go Bad

Business is great, your market share is growing, your shareholders are happy, life is good. Then one day you wake up and all hell has broken loose. Something has gone horribly wrong, the media is baying for your blood, and your customers are turning against you in droves or, worse, dropping like flies. And that brand name you built up over the years with millions of dollars' worth of advertising has turned into a scarlet letter of shame, if not an actual criminal indictment.

Most brands lead a quiet life of advance and retreat in the public eye, never touched by the adrenaline of scandal. But a few, whether through lack of foresight, corporate malfeasance, or simple bad luck, explode into the top of the national newscasts, and the news is never good for the companies in such cases. Some eventually recover, some quietly disappear, and some assume new identities hoping to shake the taint of disaster.

Below are a few of the higher profile brand disasters (or near disasters) of recent years:

Kool-Aid—In 1978, Peoples Temple cult leader Jim Jones forced more than nine hundred followers at his Jonestown compound in Guyana to commit suicide by drinking cyanide-laced Flavor-Aid, a drink mix similar to Kool-Aid. Although Kool-Aid was in no way involved in the Jonestown tragedy, errors in news media reporting and public misconceptions cast a pall, albeit mild and brief, over the product. Today the only remnant of the spurious Jonestown Kool-Aid connection is the popular catch phrase "drink the Kool-Aid," meaning "to believe absurd PR claims and become a true believer." Kool-Aid probably isn't thrilled, but it could have been a lot worse.

Pinto—On the instructions of Lee Iacocca, president of the Ford Motor Company in 1971 when the car was introduced, "The Pinto was not to weigh an ounce over 2,000 pounds and not cost a cent over $2,000." That turned out to be the formula for perhaps the most famous automotive death trap ever built. Ford engineers were later shown to have cut corners and compromised passenger safety, possibly with the knowledge of management, in designing the compact car, and it quickly became famous for bursting into flames when struck from the rear. In 1978, Ford finally agreed to recall 1.5 million Pintos for fuel-tank defects, by which time the Pinto had long since become the fodder for grisly jokes. Although the Pinto (Spanish for "painted") was named for the American pinto horse breed that dates back to the sixteenth century, the name Pinto was apparently so tainted by the exploding Fords that no major product uses it today.

Prunes—It's not really a brand, but prunes do have an industry association (the California Prune Board) that decided a few years ago that prunes had a major image problem. Long associated in the popular mind with older people eating them for their laxative properties, prunes were languishing while other fruits were enjoying a boom market among the health-conscious. So the Prune Board petitioned the FDA, and in June 2000 it became legal to call prunes "dried plums" (which is, after all, what they are). And the California Prune Board even got to change its moniker to the California Dried Plum Board, although, sadly, prune juice doesn't get a new name. "Dried plum juice" would just be too weird.

Tylenol—The case of the Tylenol murders shows that a brand beset by disaster can be saved if the company is not at fault and takes dramatic steps to limit the damage. In 1982 seven people in the Chicago area died after taking Tylenol painkiller capsules that had been laced with cyanide by persons unknown. Within days the maker of Tylenol, Johnson & Johnson, shut down production of the drug and recalled every Tylenol capsule in the nation, 31 million bottles in all with a value of more than $100 million. After it was proven that only a few bottles in the Chicago area had been tampered with, Johnson & Johnson set out to rehabilitate the Tylenol brand with new tamperproof packaging and a PR campaign that included sending free samples of the new bottle to any consumer who asked for one. "I don't think they can ever sell another product under that name," advertising guru Jerry Della Femina had declared a few days after the poisonings, but he was proven wrong.

Within a few months, Johnson & Johnson, by putting public safety above profits and taking quick action to prevent future tampering, had saved the Tylenol brand.

ValuJet—On May 11, 1996, discount airline ValuJet's Flight 592 crashed in the Florida Everglades, killing all 110 passengers and crew on board. The horrific nature of the crash and subsequent wrongful death lawsuits alleging safety violations made the name ValuJet worse than valueless in the air passenger market. So in 1997 ValuJet acquired another airline named AirTran, changed its own corporate name to AirTran, and repainted its remaining airplanes. AirTran's Web site today makes no mention of ValuJet.

WorldCom—Now you see it, now you don't, they hope. Way back in 1983, Bernie Ebbers and some friends in Hattiesburg, Mississippi, started a company by the prosaic name of Long Distance Discount Service, or LDDS. Come 1995 and a few corporate acquisitions, LDDS changed its name to WorldCom. Two years later it merged with the high-profile long-distance carrier MCI. Everyone loved WorldCom, and its stock soared.

In 2001, the bubble burst and Bernie and the boys were caught inflating WorldCom's books by $11 billion, leading to the largest corporate bankruptcy in history. Bernie and his friends were indicted for numerous bad things. WorldCom was now the butt of Jay Leno jokes and poison in the market, which was a problem because the company deeply wanted to stay in business (a prospect the average American viewed as something akin to Lizzie Borden becoming a family therapist). What to do? Simple. WorldCom adopted the name of its subsidiary MCI and moved from Mississippi to Virginia. Since most consumers never knew that MCI was part of WorldCom, the tactic seems to have worked so far. But if more skeletons come tumbling out of the closet, maybe it should just change its name to Alias Industries.

There was a time, when ocean liners were the only way to cross the Atlantic, when the origin of the name Life Savers would have seemed obvious. But in a sense the whole story really revolves around the weather in Cleveland, Ohio.

Clarence Crane was a candy maker in Cleveland in 1912, doing well with his line of chocolates, but Crane had a problem. In fact, all of Cleveland had a problem in the years before air-conditioning became common. The summers in the city were so hot and humid that chocolate candy became chocolate glop that no one wanted to buy. To a candy maker like Crane, this made summer a definite dud.

So Crane set out to invent a "summer candy" that wouldn't melt. Hard candy mints at that time were almost all imported from Europe, little square pillow-shaped things that came in cardboard tubes. Crane's inspiration was to hire a pill maker to press his candies into the novel doughnut shape. Noting the resemblance his new mints bore to the classic life preserver flotation rings carried on the passenger boats of the day, Crane christened them Life Savers and even embossed the name on one side, the way a ship's life preservers would be marked. After registering his trademark, Crane then sold the whole shebang (for just $2,900) to Edward Noble, who subsequently designed the foil-wrapped roll package that is still used today.

Lipton

Even if Thomas Lipton had never touched a drop of tea, he would probably still be famous as an early genius of marketing.

Returning to his native Scotland in 1870 at age twenty-one after a spell in America, Lipton opened his own grocery shop in Glasgow.

For the time, Lipton was an energetically innovative salesman. He used a variety of spectacular stunts to grab public attention and lure customers, including hiding gold coins in a huge cheese he had commissioned, lending the frantic air of a lottery to his formerly ho-hum cheese sales.

But it was on a trip to Australia that Lipton's nose for a good idea produced his real jackpot. Stopping off en route in Ceylon, Lipton bought five tea plantations and was soon importing the tea to Scotland. More important, Lipton decided to sell the tea, until then sold only in bulk form, in small prepackaged packets. Lipton's no-muss, no-fuss packets were an instant hit, with more than four million sold the first year, and the name Lipton quickly became synonymous with tea.

M&Ms

Some parents kick their kids out of the house. Frank Mars kicked his son out of the country.

In the beginning, there was Franklin Mars, who started a small candy company in Tacoma, Washington, in 1911. In 1923, Mars, by then in Minneapolis, Minnesota, invented the Milky Way candy bar, which became a national hit and was soon followed by his equally successful Three Musketeers and Snickers bars.

By 1928, Mars' son, Forrest, had graduated from Yale and

joined the family business. But Forrest and his father did not get along, and finally the elder Mars presented Forrest with a proposition he couldn't refuse: take the recipe and foreign rights to the Milky Way bar and leave the country. Forrest skedaddled to England and started his own candy company, churning out Milky Ways for an appreciative British public. As a sideline, he also started England's first pet food company, replacing the table scraps on which British pets had, until then, subsisted.

In 1939, as World War II gathered steam in Europe, Forrest Mars returned to the United States, bringing with him the American rights to a British candy called Smarties, small circular tablets of chocolate coated in a shell of hard candy. To sell his new product, Mars went into partnership with R. Bruce Murric, who just happened to be the adopted son of chocolate magnate Milton Hershey. Unfortunately, there already was candy named Smarties in the market in the United States, a small, tart confection sold in a roll, so Mars and Murric needed a new name. In renaming Smarties for the American market, Mars simply combined his last initial with that of his partner, Murrie, and "M&Ms" was born.

Originally sold in paper tubes, M&Ms were an instant hit, especially because they didn't melt during the summer when candy sales traditionally slumped, due to their "meltproof" hard candy shell. That shell also made M&Ms a natural choice for the U.S. Army to issue to its soldiers as part of standard rations during the war, and in 1954 Mars adopted the slogan "The milk chocolate melts in your mouth—not in your hand," which is still used today.

After his father's death in 1934, Forrest fought a long legal battle to take control of Mars, Inc., finally succeeding in 1962. Today Mars manufactures M&Ms, Milky Way, Snickers, Three Musketeers, and other candy as well as Uncle Ben's Rice (which Forrest Mars perfected), and Kal Kan and Pedigree pet foods. Kicking his son out of the country may have been the best business decision Frank Mars ever made.

Maxwell House

Joel Cheek was a little obsessed with coffee. Working as a traveling salesman, Cheek sold a variety of groceries, but it was with coffee that he spent his spare time, trying different mixtures and convinced that eventually he would come up with a better blend than those on the market.

Apparently, Cheek was right. In 1892, Cheek convinced the management of one of Nashville's best hotels, the Maxwell House, to give his latest blend a try. The reaction of Maxwell House guests to the new coffee was so enthusiastic that the hotel owner decreed that no other brand be served in his dining room, and Maxwell House brand coffee was born.

A few years later, in 1907, President Theodore Roosevelt was staying at The Hermitage, the historic Nashville residence of Andrew Jackson. Served a cup of Maxwell House coffee, Roosevelt proclaimed it "Good to the last drop," thereby providing Cheek and his company with an endorsement to die for and a slogan still used by Maxwell House today.

A minor and not entirely serious ruckus, however, erupted

at the time when a few pundits pointed out that the standard meaning of *to* in such a context was "up until," raising the question of what was wrong with that last drop in Roosevelt's cup. Only when a Columbia University English professor was enlisted to testify that *to* in this case could also mean "including" did the pundits quiet down and drink their coffee.

McDonald's

McDonald's may well be the most famous global corporation with a family name, but the McDonald brothers actually had little to do with the success of their namesake.

Dick and Maurice (Mac) McDonald had a small restaurant in San Bernardino, California, in 1954, selling 15-cent hamburgers and milkshakes to a drive-in crowd. The McDonald brothers' business was booming, as evidenced by the fact that they were running eight five-spindle milkshake mixers (called Multimixers) at once.

Meanwhile, a fifty-two-year-old salesman named Ray Kroc had just mortgaged his house and invested his life savings to become the exclusive distributor for the Multimixer, and he decided to pay his customers the McDonalds a visit. Kroc was impressed with the speed and efficiency of the McDonalds' operation and immediately sealed a partnership deal in which he would open branches of "McDonald's" restaurants around the United States. The first franchised McDonald's opened in Des Plaines, Illinois, in 1955, was an immediate hit and eventually blossomed into a global empire of 28,000 McDonald's restaurants in 119 countries. Unfortunately, the McDonald brothers had sold Ray Kroc the exclusive rights to the name "McDonald's" back in 1961, so they never got a nibble of the profits from the "billions and billions" of McDonald's burgers sold since then.

Mentos

First manufactured in 1932 by the Dutch candy making firm of Van Melle, this powerful, chewy mint sold in rolls is now known primarily for a series of TV spots that began in the 1990s and have alternately been described as "bizarre," "brilliant," and simply "the world's most annoying commercials."

In a typical Mentos commercial, a young couple in a sidewalk café has no luck catching the waiter's eye to place an order. The young man pops a Mentos in his mouth and is instantly inspired. Rising from his seat, he transforms himself into a waiter by wrapping the tablecloth around his waist and marches up to the counter. On his way back with their order, he is spotted by the real waiter, whose annoyance is replaced by a smile when he sees the young man pop another Mentos. There is, the waiter knows, no arguing with the power of "The Freshmaker"! If there is a unifying theme to Mentos commercials, it seems to be that you can get away with nearly any social transgression by waving a roll of the candies, a sort of "non compos Mentos" defense.

The name Mentos seems a genuine mystery. Mentos were

conceived during a journey of brothers Michael and Pierre van Melle to Poland in 1932, when Pierre had, as the company puts it, "a vision of peppermint-flavored caramel candy to go by the name of Mentos," but "mentos" is not a Polish word. The Dutch word for *mint* is *munt*, and "mentos" is not a word in Dutch or German. The French *menton* means "chin," which certainly moves when chewing Mentos, but in all likelihood the van Melle brothers simply invented the name.

Milk Duds

At least they didn't call them Milk Screwups. When Chicago candy maker F. Hoffman & Company set out to market chocolate-covered caramels in the early 1900s, it decided to aim high and make them perfectly spherical little balls. Unfortunately, Hoffman's chefs soon discovered that, try as they might, their perfect little chocolate caramel balls always came out little chocolate caramel lumps. Hoffman & Co. decided to market its lumpy candy anyway, and picked the name Milk Duds, referring to their high milk content and their less-than-perfect shape. Fortunately, the public wasn't looking for geometric perfection in candy, and Milk Duds were an immediate hit. Now produced by Hershey Foods, Milk Duds have been popular ever since.

Mountain Dew

You'd never guess it from the extreme dudes and cool chicks who exhort America's youth to "Do the Dew!" in its raucous ads, but Mountain Dew was born in the sleepy hills and hollers of Tennessee in the 1940s. Early Mountain Dew bottles featured Willy the Hillbilly, accompanied by his pet pig, taking a potshot at a fleeing revenuer. The design of the bottle, according to the company's official history, was "intended to make the product feel like the illegally made liquor cooked up in mountain stills."

In fact, when brothers Barney and Ally Hartman, owners of a Knoxville bottling company, trademarked the name Mountain Dew (long a slang term for moonshine), what they were selling was a lemon-lime mixer for whiskey, not the high-caffeine citrus soft drink the company finally perfected in the late 1950s. But soon after Pepsi-Cola bought the company in 1964, Mountain Dew abandoned Willy the Hillbilly, and today Dew advertising is targeted squarely at what the company describes as "young, active, outdoor types" who are presumably too busy snowboarding to shoot at revenuers.

Ore-Ida

Chances are that Nephi and Golden Grigg thought potatoes were about the simplest product going when they founded their frozen french fry company in 1951. The Grigg brothers had already bought a frozen-foods factory in Ontario, Oregon, and had potato fields in Burley, Idaho. Now all they needed was a name for their company.

The name, as it turned out, was staring at them from their own addresses, and they decided to dub the company Ore-Ida, simply combining *Ore*gon and *Ida*ho. Ore-Ida began marketing frozen french fries immediately, but in 1953 a new product was developed that would lift Ore-Ida out of the ranks of frozen-food manufacturers and would go into the pantheon of American comfort foods. Soon Ore-Ida's Tater Tots (*tot* being an eighteenth-century term for a small amount of anything), small breaded chunks of seasoned shredded potato, were cropping up on school lunch menus across the land and burrowing their way into the consciousness (and arteries) of the baby boom generation.

Ore-Ida was acquired in 1965 by the H. J. Heinz Company, which began to aggressively promote the brand with the slogan "When it says Ore-Ida, it's all-righta." Today Ore-Ida is the leading brand of potato products in the United States, and Tater Tots come in onion, crispy, and "mini" varieties as well as the original form. Like White Castle hamburgers and other foods that inspire weird culinary creativity among their fans, Tater Tots have inspired some fairly far-fetched recipes. The winner of a recent official contest was apparently a concoction called Pineapple Cranberry Tater Tot Pudding, the recipe for which ends with the observation that the dish can be "served with whipped cream or ice cream if desired." That sound you hear is your guests pulling out of your driveway.

Oreo

Maybe some things are just not meant to be known by mortal man. Or maybe the origin of the name Oreo is subject to the Heisenberg Uncertainty Principle, as subatomic particles are, and if we ever nailed down the name, the cookies wouldn't taste as good. Or maybe the folks who invented the cookie were just too busy stuffing their faces at the time to take notes.

What we do know is that Oreos, two chocolate wafers with a creamy filling, were invented in New York City in 1912 and known at first as Oreo Biscuits. (Many cookies were called biscuits at that time, and still are in the U.K.)

From there, the Oreo became the Oreo Sandwich, then the Oreo Creme Sandwich, and finally the Oreo Chocolate Sandwich Cookie. Today Nabisco produces, in addition to the classic Oreo, a dizzying array of Oreo variations, including Fudge Covered Oreos, Chocolate Creme Oreos, Double Delight Oreos, Double Stuf Oreos, Fudge Mint Covered Oreos, Mini Fudge Oreos, Mini Chocolate Creme Oreos, Reduced Fat Oreos, and White Fudge Covered Oreos.

None of which explains where the name Oreo came from, to which the Official Nabisco Answer (so don't yell at me) is: Sorry, nobody knows. The only crumb of etymological hope is a theory that the early Oreos were shaped like a dome or hill, and that the name came from the Greek *oreo,* which means "mountain." Or maybe Oreo was just easy to say and remember.

Ovaltine

You may never have actually tasted it, but chances are you've heard of it, and chances are that you've also wondered, along with millions of children in the past century, "What *is* that stuff?"

Ovaltine is a chocolaty drink made from malt extract. In the late nineteenth century, a Swiss scientist named Georg Wander invented a process of easily extracting a nutritious syrup from malted barley of the sort used to make beer. Wander believed that he had discovered, in his malt extract, a possible solution to the scourge of malnutrition, or at least a healthful supplement to the average diet.

Perhaps he had, but the problem was that no one was interested in eating Dr. Wander's goo. His son Albert, however, realized that if he mixed the malt extract with sugar, whey, beet extract, and eggs, people would be interested in at least trying the stuff. Albert marketed his product as a powder and called it "Ovomaltine," from the eggs (in Latin, *ovo*) and malt it contained. Served hot as an energy drink at Swiss ski resorts, Ovomaltine was an instant hit and was subsequently exported all over Europe. When it hit the U.K. in 1904, it was sold under the shortened name Ovaltine, and it was Ovaltine that shortly thereafter took America by storm. By this time, the chocolate flavor of Ovaltine had crowded out all the other varieties, and it was advertised as the hot chocolate drink that was good for you.

Ovaltine was a huge success on both sides of the Atlantic

largely because of an aggressive and clever advertising campaign of sponsoring children's radio shows. In the U.K. in 1939, more than five million children were members of a club based on a radio serial called *The League of Ovaltineys*. In the United States, Ovaltine sponsored both *Little Orphan Annie* and *Captain Midnight,* as well as several popular TV shows in the 1950s. And for Mom and Dad, folklore held that Ovaltine, mixed with raw eggs, was a powerful aphrodisiac.

Sadly, as the Ovaltine generation aged, sales slumped, and Ovaltine has in recent years been passed from one owner to another. Perhaps most tellingly, it appears that Ovaltine, once touted as a high-energy pick-me-up, is now viewed by the public as a bedtime sleep aid.

Peeps

There's really no mystery about why Peeps, the little marshmallow candy critters that magically appear on store shelves as holidays (especially Easter) approach, are called Peeps. The original Peeps were molded in the shape of little birds, and little birds generally make a *peep peep* noise. Linguists call the word *peep* an echoic (or onomatopoetic, if you're feeling fancy) formation, meaning that *peep* derived not from some solemn Latin term like *peepus annoyus* but from somebody's simple attempt to imitate a little bird. But that doesn't mean Peeps haven't had an interesting history, one that began, in fact, with a pun.

The Peeps saga began in 1910, when Russian candy maker

Sam Born arrived in New York City from France. Sam was an inventive guy, and within a few years had pioneered several innovations in the candy trade, including chocolate sprinkles (or jimmies) and the hard chocolate coating on ice cream bars. Sam also understood the new role of technology in revolutionizing the candy business to serve a mass market. In 1916, he was presented with the keys to the city of San Francisco for inventing a machine that would automatically insert the sticks in lollipops.

In 1917, Sam Born opened a candy store in New York City, and emphasized the freshness of his candies (not to mention his own name) with signs proclaiming "Just Born!" In 1923, Sam Born founded his own wholesale candy manufacturing company in Brooklyn, New York, and called it, of course, Just Born, Inc. In 1932, Just Born moved its operations to Bethlehem, Pennsylvania.

In 1953, Just Born acquired the Rodda Candy Company, a noted jellybean maker. But while jellybeans were popular, Just Born was especially interested in the small line of marshmallow candies Rodda had been making, including Easter Peeps, small yellow birds produced by laboriously hand-squeezing marshmallow through a pastry tube. Within a year, Just Born had mechanized the Peeps process, and began cranking out and marketing Peeps by the millions.

With Peeps becoming ubiquitous at Easter, it seemed silly to ignore other holidays, and by the 1960s Just Born was producing marshmallow snowmen for Christmas and pumpkins and cats for Halloween. Today Peeps come in all shapes (bunnies, eggs, hearts, and, of course, chocolate bats), colors (including lavender and patriotic Peeps in red, white, and blue) and sizes (thus fulfilling mankind's ancient quest for a giant marshmallow bunny).

Pepperidge Farm

Like many New York City dwellers, Margaret Fogarty Rudkin dreamed of someday leaving the city for the simple country life. Unlike most, she not only made the move but founded a multimillion-dollar business in her new rural home.

Together with her husband and two young sons, Rudkin bought land near Fairfield, Connecticut, built a house, and named their new homestead Pepperidge Farm for the pepper trees that dotted their property. The Rudkins threw themselves into the farm life, raising vegetables and fruits and livestock. In 1937, when one of her sons became sick, Rudkin set out to develop her own special all-natural high-nutrition bread for him. When her son's doctor tasted the bread, he declared it delicious and asked for some for himself. Soon Rudkin's neighbors were enthusiastically insisting that she produce the bread for sale, and Rudkin suddenly found herself in the mail-order bread business.

Sales to local grocers boomed, and in 1947 the Rudkins opened a commercial bakery in Norwalk. By 1953, Pepperidge Farm was producing 77,000 loaves per week, and in 1968 the business Margaret Rudkin had started in her kitchen was acquired by the Campbell Soup Company. Not bad, one might say, for city slickers.

Pepsi-Cola

It's fair to say that if there had been no Coca-Cola, there might still be a Pepsi-Cola, but it might well be called something else.

Pepsi-Cola was invented in 1898, twelve years after the debut of Coca-Cola, by pharmacist Caleb D. Bradham of New Bern, North Carolina. (Coke had been invented in Atlanta, Georgia, in 1886 by John Pemberton, also a pharmacist. The role of pharmacists of the southern United States in developing soft drinks would seem to be a fertile topic for doctoral dissertations.)

The invention and widespread marketing of Coca-Cola a few years earlier had spurred the appearance of numerous competing cola-based beverages with similar names, including Cold Cola, Candy Cola, the odd Cay-Ola, and the unfortunately named Fig Cola, many of which were later ruled to be infringements on Coca-Cola's trademark.

Perhaps mindful of the confusion caused by this cola rush, Bradham at first called his creation simply Brad's Drink. But apparently that name turned out to be a little too bland to catch the eye of cola fans, and in short order Bradham joined the "-Cola" club. Since he had originally developed the drink as a remedy for upset stomachs (dyspepsia), the name Pepsi-Cola, with its added connotation of pep and vigor, was a logical choice, and the new brand name was trademarked in 1903.

Pillsbury

It is unlikely that in 1872, when Charles Pillsbury founded the baking products company that bears his name, he foresaw that someday his moniker would be largely associated with a small animated character with an annoying giggle.

Charles and his father, George, had joined with his uncle John Pillsbury to operate a milling plant in 1869, and Charles had used his share of the profits to start C. A. Pillsbury and Company, which sold cereal and baking products with increasing success from the late nineteenth to the mid-twentieth century.

But it was in 1965 that Pillsbury graduated from a grocery store staple brand to a pop culture sensation with the introduction in company commercials of Poppin' Fresh, aka the Pillsbury Doughboy. Dispatched to push Pillsbury's line of refrigerated cookie and biscuit doughs, Poppin' Fresh, a diminutive humanoid blob of dough sporting a cheery smile and a chef's hat, was within three years recognized by an astounding 87 percent of all consumers and is today consistently rated as the number one food character, beating out such luminaries as Starkist's Charlie the Tuna and the Green Giant. Poppin' Fresh's signature giggling falsetto was created for the initial series of commercials by the legendary voice actor Paul Frees, previously known as the gravelly Russian voice of Boris Badenov on TV's *The Rocky and Bullwinkle Show*.

One measure of Poppin' Fresh's success is that few consumers probably remember that until his appearance, *dough-*

boy was heard only as an antiquated slang term for a soldier or infantryman. There is controversy about the origin of *dough-boy* in the military sense, but one certainty is that the term is much older than most people would suspect. Although it gained currency in popular use during World War I, *doughboy* first showed up in print in 1847, and General George Armstrong Custer's widow mentioned the term in her memoirs, written in 1887, explaining that "doughboys" were small doughnuts often served to sailors aboard ship. According to Mrs. Custer, the term was subsequently applied to infantrymen because the large brass buttons on their uniforms reminded someone of these naval doughboys. Lending support to at least the culinary aspect of Mrs. Custer's theory is the fact that *doughboy* has meant "a boiled flour dumpling" to sailors since about 1685.

Pringles

Well, one thing's for certain: it was a lot cheaper than hiring some fancy naming consultant, and it seems to have worked.

Casting around for a name for their new "potato snack product" in the late 1960s, the marketing folks at Procter & Gamble had a thought. Instead of trying to dream up a completely new name, why not take a close look at the names that already exist? So they pulled out the phone book for their hometown of Cincinnati, Ohio, and started browsing.

Some time later (exactly how much later is not recorded, but Cincinnati is a pretty big town), they hit the jackpot.

Tucked away in the suburb of Finneytown, they found a street named Pringle Avenue. Pringle . . . Potato. That's it! Pringles Potato Snack Product! No, wait, let's call them "Crisps." And so perfectly round Pringles Potato Crisps hit America's streets in 1968, neatly stacked in a distinctive cylindrical metal can.

Pringles are still going strong today, available in a wide range of flavors, including original Pringles, Sweet Mesquite BBQ, Sour Cream & Onion, Pizza-licious, and Salt & Vinegar. There's even a Pringles-inspired tortilla chip called Torengos, which are perfectly triangular and come in, what else, a triangular cylindrical can.

Red Baron Pizza

Oh what a tangled web we weave when a product name we do conceive. For the makers of one of America's most popular brands of frozen pizza, the folks at Red Baron Pizza adopt an oddly defensive tone when asked how their product's name was chosen.

To many of us (especially history and aviation aficionados), the name Red Baron must certainly refer to Baron Manfred Freiherr von Richthofen, the ace German fighter pilot of World War I. At the dawn of the age of air combat, the Red Baron (so named for his bright red Fokker triplane) blasted a total of eighty British, French, and American aircraft from the sky, becoming a legend on both sides of the conflict before being shot down and killed in 1918.

The connection between the German fighter and Red

Baron frozen pizza seems even more obvious in light of the company's logo. The "Red Baron character," a ruggedly handsome fellow, sports a World War I–vintage leather flying helmet and goggles, a dashing mustache above a chiseled chin, and a flowing red scarf of the kind worn by early aviators.

But the folks at Red Baron are adamant that the dashing chap on the box is not *that* Red Baron: "The Red Baron character was selected in 1976 as the Red Baron pizza icon to represent Schwan's Sales Enterprises entrance into a new frontier—the frozen pizza category. Red Baron Pizza took creative license with the character; he is not modeled after the actual German 'Red Baron' Manfred Freiherr von Richthofen of the WWI era."

"Not modeled after" is, of course, open to interpretation. If I were to don tights and a cape, I might not be *modeling* myself on Superman, but surely at least a little homage is going on. But such distancing is understandable. Naming a product aimed at American consumers after a German war hero is clearly a risky business decision.

So Red Baron Pizza, while denying a direct connection to Richthofen, stresses the more laudable aspects of the flying ace's legend: "The Baron represents not only the sense of adventure and quality that every Red Baron product brings to family life but also the brand's pursuit of excellence." That fellow on the box, you see, represents the pursuit of *excellence*, not the pursuit of British and American *airplanes*.

Apart from the Richthofen-pepperoni axis, however, another odd coincidence seems to haunt the Red Baron story. Perhaps not surprisingly, the "Red Baron character" on the pizza box bears little physical resemblance to Baron von Richthofen, who lacked a mustache and appears from photographs to have been rather narrow-shouldered and slight of stature. The pizza-box Red Baron, in contrast, is a near doppelgänger of Hollywood hunk Tom Selleck. But the Red Baron pizza folks are not amused by that comparison either, firmly declaring that "Red Baron Pizza took creative license with the Red Baron character; he is not modeled after a celebrity."

In any case, the Schwan Food Company, makers of Red Baron Pizza, have put the pizza-aviation connection to good use. The Red Baron squadron, a company-sponsored fleet of World War-II era open-cockpit Stearman biplanes, appears at air shows throughout the United States and has raised millions of dollars for children's charities since 1979.

Sara Lee

"Everybody doesn't like something, but nobody doesn't like Sara Lee." It was a catchy slogan set to a catchy tune (penned by Mitch Leigh, of *Man of La Mancha* fame) when it was introduced in 1968, and today is considered one of the most successful ad jingles ever. But it never explained who Sara Lee was.

As it happens, Sara Lee Lubin was the daughter of Charles Lubin, who owned a chain of bakeries in Chicago in the 1930s. Lubin tested his recipes on his daughter, and eventually renamed his bakeries Kitchens of Sara Lee.

In the 1950s, the Sara Lee Corporation pioneered the sales

of frozen baked goods, and today, in addition to its food line, owns a slew of other brands, including Hanes, Bali, Wonderbra, Playtex, Polo Ralph Lauren, DKNY, Kiwi shoe care products, Brylcreem, and something called Mister Turkey.

Sara Lee herself hasn't played a role in the company since she was a teenager, and today, a grandmother, she is said to be a computer whiz.

7-UP

C. L. Grigg was one determined inventor. In 1920, Grigg, who had worked in advertising and marketing for thirty years, founded the Howdy Corporation in St. Louis, Missouri, to manufacture and market an orange-flavored drink he had come up with and named Howdy Orange Soda. Howdy did well, but Grigg had a dream, a dream of inventing a more distinctive soft drink that would grab the consumer by the lapels and not let go. So Grigg set out in search of his dream soda pop. And he searched, and searched, and then he searched some more. In the end, he spent more than two years developing and testing (on whom is unclear) eleven different kinds of lemon-flavored concoctions. Finally, in October 1929, he was satisfied with the result and ready to debut his new lemon-lime drink to a thirsty public.

Unfortunately, not only were the Fates not smiling on Grigg, they actually seemed to be laughing at him, and his new brand was hit with a triple whammy right out of the gate. The date he picked to introduce his new drink was exactly two weeks before the 1929 stock market crash, an event that doubt-less drove many people to drink, but not soda pop. Second, the unwieldy name Grigg had picked for his new soft drink—Bib-Label Lithiated Lemon-Lime Soda—made the name Howdy Orange Soda sound like poetry. (*Lithiated,* by the way, means "impregnated with a salt of lithium.") Third, there were al-ready more than six hundred other lemon-lime soft drinks on the market, many of them with names that didn't sound like escapees from chemistry class.

There was actually a fourth factor: Grigg had chosen to use caramel coloring to make his soda brown, not a color usually associated with lemon-lime flavor. Oddly enough, consumers didn't seem put off by the color, the name, the stock market, or the competition, and Grigg's Bib-Label Lithiated Lemon-Lime Soda was a modest hit with the public. This apparently gave Grigg enough breathing space to reconsider the wisdom of that Bib-Label Lithiated moniker, and in record time he had renamed his drink 7-UP, describing it by way of explanation as "seven natural flavors blended into a savory, flavory drink with a real wallop."

The name change (and the subsequent dropping of caramel coloring in favor of a "clear" look) apparently did the trick, and by 1940, C. L. Grigg's 7-UP was the third-most pop-ular soft drink in the world.

SPAM

Just when we were all getting used to the convenience of e-mail, the down side popped up with a vengeance: mountains of spam clogging our electronic mailboxes. "Spam" is Internet jargon for unsolicited junk e-mail, the obnoxious get-rich-quick schemes, V*I*A*G*R*A* pitches, and other commercial messages sent out in the millions every day by bulk-mail spammers. But this negative use of *spam* isn't really fair to the original SPAM.

SPAM is the registered trademark (always spelled in all capital letters) for a canned lunch meat, made from pork shoulders and ham, invented by George Hormel & Co. in 1937. Hormel needed a name for its new product and, rather than hire someone to come up with one, decided to kill two birds with a naming contest that would also garner some free publicity. Kenneth Daigneau, an actor (and brother of a Hormel vice president), suggested "SPAM," which he explained was short for "spiced ham." Bingo. Daigneau took home the $100 prize, which even today buys you more SPAM than any rational person would be likely to want.

SPAM was nearly the perfect product for its time when it was introduced. Meat of any kind had been hard to come by in the Great Depression of the 1930s, and during World War II, SPAM, with its long shelf life and durable can, became a staple for soldiers and civilians alike all over the world. Even Premier Nikita Krushchev credited SPAM with saving the lives of Soviet soldiers during the war. All told, more than five billion cans of

SPAM have been produced, enough to circle the globe almost thirteen times.

Hormel today produces traditional SPAM, SPAM Lite, SPAM Smoke Flavored, SPAM Less Sodium, and even SPAM Oven Roasted Turkey.

Spam in its more recent junk e-mail sense owes its origin to Monty Python's classic 1970 "SPAM" sketch, in which a couple discovers that the restaurant they've chosen for breakfast serves SPAM with everything, like it or not. (Woman: "Have you got anything without SPAM?" Waitress: "Well, there's SPAM, egg, sausage, and SPAM. That's not got much SPAM in it.") To Python-literate Net users, the inescapable tsunami of junk e-mail that swamped the Net in the mid-nineties naturally conjured up the skit's chorus of Vikings (don't ask) singing "SPAM, SPAM, lovely SPAM" over and over again.

Hormel isn't thrilled with this derogatory usage of spam, but acts legally only if someone tries to trademark a product name that includes the word *spam*. As the eminently reasonable and surprisingly tolerant folks at Hormel put it, "Ultimately, we are trying to avoid the day when the consuming public asks, 'Why would Hormel Foods name its product after junk e-mail?' "

Starbucks

No sooner had the Mars rover started beaming back pictures of the desolate Martian landscape to Earth than a digitally-altered version of the picture began making the e-mail rounds on the

Internet. To the sand dunes and red rocks had been added one tiny, inevitable improvement visible in the distance: a Starbucks coffee shop.

Generally credited with popularizing high-quality coffee and pricey boutique coffee concoctions in the United States in the late 1980s and 1990s, Starbucks is perhaps equally famous for its dizzying ubiquity. Starbucks cafés in Manhattan now seem to outnumber bus stops, and even supermarkets in rural Ohio have begun to sprout Starbucks stands squeezed between the produce section and the photofinishing counter.

With more than 7,225 stores worldwide, Starbucks is well on its way to becoming a global household name, but the name Starbucks itself may strike some customers as slightly myste-rious. There has never been anyone by that name associated with the company, and while the two syllables—*star* and *bucks*—are forceful and memorable, neither has any intrinsic connection to the business (apart from, in the case of *bucks*, as fodder for cynical puns). The name Starbucks, however, will ring a bell with students of American literature.

When writer Gordon Bowker and teachers Jerry Baldwin and Zev Siegel founded Starbucks in Seattle in 1971, they were aiming to replicate the success of the legendary Peets Coffee and Tea in Berkeley, California, by creating a local market for high-quality imported coffees. According to Starbucks company lore, the name is drawn from Starbuck, the coffee-loving first mate in Herman Melville's classic novel *Moby-Dick*. The founders felt that a seafaring reference would conjure up images of the exotic days of the early coffee trade, and the first Starbucks store was, in fact, outfitted with a nautical decor and fixtures.

The Starbucks logo as well followed a nautical theme from the beginning, featuring a mermaid (strictly adhering to the mythological definition, which included a split tail) wearing a crown, but has undergone significant modification since the company's early days. The original's bare breasts have been covered, and her split tail, considered sexually suggestive by some customers, has been largely cropped from the logo.

Twinkies

For an innocent, remarkably wholesome snack food, Twinkies get no respect. A Web page called The T.W.I.N.K.I.E.S. Project (www.twinkiesproject.com) purports to investigate the effect on Twinkies of, among other tortures, being doused with flaming alcohol and being tossed from a sixth-floor window. The "researchers" even claim that the name of their project stands for Tests With Inorganic Noxious Kakes In Extreme Situations.

Noxious? Twinkies are actually made with standard ingredients (milk, eggs, etc.) and are baked.

More well known bad publicity resulted from the 1978 shooting of San Francisco mayor George Moscone and city supervisor Harvey Milk by Dan White, a former city official. White's attorneys argued that he was suffering from depression and diminished mental capacity, states evidenced by his steady diet of Twinkies and other junk food. While the argument was never made that Twinkies actually *caused* the murders, White's acquittal on murder charges catapulted the term "Twinkie defense" into the public eye as a synonym for refusing to take responsibility for one's acts.

All of this is seen as terribly unfair by Twinkies aficionados, who point out that those little golden tube cakes were developed during the Depression, when inexpensive treats were hard to come by. Jimmy Dewar, manager of the Schiller Park, Illinois, Hostess bakery, had noticed that the pans used to bake Hostess's Little Shortbread Fingers were used only during the summer. Dewar decided to come up with a use for the pans during their down period, and filled them with golden sponge cake, adding a filling after baking. Bingo, a new snack product. But Dewar still needed a name for his creation. And that's when Divine Intervention (to hear Twinkies fans tell it) appeared. On the way to show off his creation to his bosses, Dewar passed a billboard for Twinkle Toe Shoes, and the name Twinkies was born.

Incidentally, Twinkies were originally filled with banana cream, but a banana shortage during World War II forced a switch to the vanilla cream today used in more than 500 million Twinkies every year.

Wendy's

Wendy's restaurants have become such an iconic fixture on the American landscape that few customers give much thought to the chain's name, although multibillion-dollar corporations going by a person's first name are rare. But with now more than six thousand Wendy's restaurants slaking the world's hunger for burgers and salads since 1969, it's worth noting that "Wendy" was a real person.

If ever a person could be said to have been born to cook burgers, Dave Thomas fit the bill. From his first job as a counterman in a diner at age twelve, Thomas loved the restaurant business, and he dropped out of school at age fifteen to work full time at a Hobby House Restaurant in Fort Wayne, Indiana. While working there, Thomas met Colonel Harland Sanders of Kentucky Fried Chicken (now KFC) fame, and in 1962 he took over the management of four failing KFC restaurants in Columbus, Ohio. Thomas rescued the restaurants and became a millionaire by age thirty-five, setting the stage for branching out on his own.

In 1969, Dave Thomas founded the first Wendy's Old-Fashioned Hamburger Restaurant, named after his daughter, in downtown Columbus, serving made-to-order burgers in an innovative old-time atmosphere complete with wooden tables and Tiffany-style lamps. A keen judge of trends, Thomas also invented the modern drive-through window.

As the chain expanded in the years following Wendy's debut, Thomas became known for his generosity and community involvement. An adoptee himself, he worked to make adoption easier and constantly stressed the need of every child for a loving family. To those who knew Dave Thomas, his activism on behalf of children and families came as no surprise. After all, he loved his daughter so much he made her a household name.

Wonder Bread

It wasn't the best thing since sliced bread. It was the first sliced bread, period.

Consumers had been slicing bread themselves for centuries, of course (the alternative being to simply gnaw on the loaf), but if you bought bread in a store before the 1930s, it came as an unsliced loaf.

Even Wonder Bread wasn't sliced at first. First marketed in 1921 by the Taggart Baking Company of Indianapolis, Indiana, the new bread was almost ready for market when the question of a name arose. Vice president Elmer Cline happened to attend a balloon race one day, and the sight of dozens of brightly colored hot air balloons filling the sky filled him with, as he later said, "wonder." Since Cline was conveniently in charge of naming the new bread, Wonder Bread was born without further ado. Cline, in fact, was so impressed with the sight of those balloons that he covered his new product's wrapper with red, yellow, and blue balloons, still the Wonder trademark package design.

One might think that a product combining balloons, bread, and a sense of wonder couldn't get any better, but in 1933 Wonder introduced the very first presliced loaf of bread to America's consumers, the instant popularity of which is reflected today in the phrase "the best thing since sliced bread."

Yoo-Hoo

Although Yoo-Hoo today is famous as the most popular cold chocolate beverage in the United States (as opposed to hot drinks such as cocoa), the Yoo-Hoo brand name actually predates the drink itself. Back in the 1920s, the Olivieri family of New Jersey owned a small business producing fresh fruit drinks under the name Tru-Fruit. Natale Olivieri wanted to market a chocolate drink but was concerned about the problem of spoilage. The solution came one day when Olivieri was watching his wife prepare and put up jars of her homemade tomato sauce, boiling the jars before sealing them. Olivieri decided to try the same preserving process with his chocolate drink, boiling the formula right in the bottles to kill any bacteria. After some experimentation (agitating the bottles during boiling turned out to be the trick), Olivieri was satisfied that the spoilage problem had been licked and was ready to put his chocolate drink on the market.

As it happened, some of the Olivieri family's fruit drinks were already being sold under the Yoo-Hoo brand label. "Yoo-hoo" itself was at that time a well-known popular shout, an interjection used to get someone's attention, roughly equivalent to "Hey you!" but with friendlier overtones. The Olivieris put their new concoction on the market as Yoo-Hoo Chocolate Drink, and it was ultimately so successful (thanks in large part to promotion by Yogi Berra and other members of the New York Yankees in the 1950s) that all the other Yoo-Hoo drinks faded into obscurity.

Yoo-Hoo, by the way, is not chocolate milk, although it does contain dairy whey and nonfat milk. It's also not a soft drink, since it's not carbonated. Yoo-Hoo today is owned by Cadbury Schweppes, who still call it just a chocolate drink.

Zima

Zima, a "clear malt beverage" first marketed by the Coors Brewing Company in 1992, is a classic case study in successful modern branding. Among other things, Zima (essentially a premium beer from which all coloring and "beery" flavor has been filtered) stands alone as a survivor of 1992, the Year of the Clear, in which a range of "clear" products (including the short-lived Pepsi Clear and the disastrous Miller Clear beer) debuted and promptly flopped within a matter of months.

According to its coiners at Lexicon Branding, Inc. (also the creators of such high-profile brands as Intel's Pentium chip and the Apple PowerBook notebook computer), *zima* is the Russian word for "winter," a good match for a cold, clear beverage that resembles vodka.

One presumes, of course, that had the Russian word for winter turned out to be something along the lines of *phudrub*, Lexicon would have looked elsewhere for inspiration. But the name Zima turned out to be so nearly ideal from a linguistic standpoint that it might have been chosen even if it meant nothing. Zima consists of two short syllables, one consonant, one vowel each, the first one stressed, with a brevity and clarity that makes the product easy to order in a crowded, noisy bar (just try shouting "Courvoisier" some time). Even its orthographic structure (the look of the letters themselves), according to Lexicon, reinforces the "light taste and simplicity" of Zima with its simple, angular forms.

We can only hope that the subgenius who came up with Miller Clear can buy Zima in whatever marketing Siberia he now resides.

CLOTHING

Abercrombie & Fitch

Known today for selling upscale clothing to a young market (as well as for its catalog, which until recently was frequently denounced for its sexually suggestive photographs), Abercrombie & Fitch is actually one of the oldest retail chains in the United States. Today's A&F, however, is a far cry from your granddaddy's favorite sporting goods store.

Abercrombie & Fitch was the creation of an odd, and ultimately unsustainable, partnership. David T. Abercrombie was, by the 1890s, a former miner, trapper, and engineer who had established a small business in Manhattan manufacturing and selling camping, hunting, and other outdoors equipment. Ezra Fitch was a successful lawyer and avid outdoor enthusiast, a passion that made him one of Abercrombie's best customers. In 1900, after much cajoling, Fitch finally convinced Abercrombie to let him buy into the business, and in 1904 the name of the enterprise officially became Abercrombie & Fitch. By 1907, however, the honeymoon was definitely over, and irreconcilable differences over the future of the business led to the breakup of the partnership. Abercrombie resigned and went back to manufacturing camping equipment, but Fitch found new partners and A&F entered the period of its greatest success.

In 1917, the Abercrombie & Fitch Co., which had been

mailing out more than fifty thousand catalogs per year, established a twelve-story sporting goods store in Manhattan, at that time the largest in the world. Abercrombie & Fitch sold equipment and clothing for every conceivable sport or outdoor pastime, from big game hunting (Teddy Roosevelt was a customer) to lawn tennis.

By the 1960s, however, many Americans were getting all the adventure they wanted from television, and Abercrombie & Fitch foundered, finally declaring bankruptcy in 1977. After an unsuccessful reopening, again as a sporting goods chain, under new ownership, Abercrombie & Fitch was bought in 1988 by The Limited, which revamped A&F's image and inventory. Gone were the shotguns and fishing lures, replaced by trendy clothing and racy imagery.

Adidas

Adolf (Adi) Dassler pretty much invented the modern sports shoe. As a twenty-year-old track enthusiast in Germany, Dassler made his first shoe, a canvas training shoe for runners, in 1920. Over the next two decades, Dassler expanded his line, and by 1937 was producing thirty models of shoes for eleven different sports. Early on, Dassler made a point of soliciting the opinions of the athletes themselves and being personally present at the sporting events in which competitors wore his shoes.

After the interruption of World War II, Dassler restarted his company and decided to register the trademark Adidas, a melding of the first syllables of his own first and last names. In 1949, he registered the company's famous three-stripes design as a trademark. By the 1960s, Adidas dominated the professional sports shoe market and began manufacturing athletic equipment and Adidas logo clothing as well.

Banana Republic

"There are no second acts in American lives," F. Scott Fitzgerald famously declared. Too bad he didn't hang around long enough to shop at Banana Republic. If he had, he'd have witnessed one of the most striking reinventions of American business history.

Back in the late 1970s, Mel Ziegler was searching for a replacement for his beloved but badly worn safari jacket. Unfortunately, it was the Age of Disco Polyester in America, and finding duds made of natural fibers was akin to looking for brown rice at Mickey D's. Finally locating the jacket he sought at a secondhand clothing store in Australia, Ziegler realized that a market existed for exotic safari-themed clothing, and in 1978 Mel and Patricia Ziegler founded their Banana Republic store and catalog business. The name was chosen to reflect the jungle theme of the brand, and the immediate popularity of the stores overshadowed the previously derogatory connotations of the term "banana republic," a reference to autocratic Central American regimes in thrall to U.S. fruit companies.

Adopting an *Out of Africa* motif, the Banana Republic stores were a cross between a clothing store and a movie set, complete with thatched huts and vintage jeeps on the sales floor, 1940s music on the sound system, and antique airplanes hanging from the ceiling. And as the Banana Republic chain grew, it single-handedly created the "adventurer look" so popular with 1980s yuppies, lending platforms at suburban train stations an air of the Australian outback.

In 1983, Banana Republic was acquired by Gap, Inc., and rapid expansion of the chain continued. But by the early 1990s, Americans apparently had all the bush vests and snakeproof wine coolers they needed, and Banana Republic sales nosedived. Only quick thinking and fancy footwork by management saved the brand. Within a few years the jeeps and huts were gone, the pith helmets ditched, and Banana Republic was reborn as today's sleek, stylish purveyor of casual clothing and accessories for young urbanites.

Gap

Assuming that most customers shopping for a new pair of jeans prefer that their pants fit properly, the choice of The Gap as the name of a youth-oriented clothing chain might seem a little odd.

But it seemed perfect back in 1969, when Donald Fisher opened the first Gap store in San Francisco. Fisher, then forty-one and a real estate developer, had received a pair of blue jeans that didn't fit, and in the course of exchanging them at a local department store, became frustrated at the store's jumbled and disorganized method of stocking its merchandise. Convinced that stacking pants neatly by size rather than style made more sense, Fisher decided to open his own store specializing in Levi's jeans. To make his shop stand out and attract a young clientele, Fisher decided to sell records alongside the blue jeans and to call the store Pants and Disks.

But the night before the store sign was to be painted, Fisher's wife, Doris, convinced him that she had a better idea. At a recent party with friends, discussion had centered on the generation gap—the disparity in ideals and values between older and younger Americans—then so much in the news. To call the new store The Gap, she felt, would naturally draw the young, rebellious customers they were targeting. Fisher was won over, and the first Gap store opened shortly thereafter, selling so many pairs of jeans in its first few months that the sideline of record sales was soon quietly dropped.

Today Gap Inc. consists of more than 4,200 Gap, Banana Republic, and Old Navy stores in the United States, the United Kingdom, Canada, France, Japan, and Germany.

Hush Puppies

Even shoes can be late bloomers in America.

In 1958, Wolverine World Wide, a Michigan company that had been tanning leather and making shoes since 1883, was about to debut a new line of suede lace-up shoes with a crepe sole designed for comfort. The only detail missing was a good name for the shoe. Company sales manager Jim Muir happened to be visiting a friend in Tennessee one day and noticed that his host quieted his barking dogs by tossing them bits of fried cornmeal. Such fried morsels, Muir learned, were called hush puppies in the South (*hush* being a verb meaning "to quiet"), and were also commonly served as a side dish at the dinner table.

In a moment of branding genius, Muir remembered that human feet had long been known in slang as "dogs," and that someone with tired and aching feet would often say his "dogs are barking." The new comfortable shoe designed to soothe tired feet would henceforth be known as Hush Puppies.

The first Hush Puppies model, the Duke (a popular dog's name) was introduced in 1958, and subsequent early styles also featured canine names such as Toby and Bozo.

Hush Puppies were popular in the 1960s but by the late 1970s had come to be considered nerdy, associated with cardigan sweaters and aging relatives. Even Wolverine's chief executive joked that Hush Puppies were the shoes that elderly widows put on their husbands in the casket, and by 1990 Wolverine was playing down its own brand.

All that changed, at least briefly, in 1994, when Tom Hanks wore Hush Puppies in the hit film *Forrest Gump*. Suddenly Hush Puppies were a fashion sensation and even celebrities had to put their names on waiting lists for the shoes.

By the late 1990s, however, the Hollywood bloom had faded and Hush Puppies sales slumped again. But there's always the possibility that this old dog may have a few more tricks, and lives, left.

Keds

If at first you don't succeed, change a consonant. But be sure to pick the right consonant.

Back in the late eighteenth century, rubber-soled canvas shoes were becoming popular in both Europe and the United States. Sure-footed, comfortable, and nearly silent compared to leather-soled boots and shoes, rubber-soled footwear even gave us the slang term "gumshoe" from the gum-rubber soled shoes favored by detectives on the prowl for miscreants.

In 1892, nine small companies joined together to form the U.S. Rubber Company. One of the member companies, the oddly named Goodyear Metallic Rubber Shoe Company, happened to hold the license to Charles Goodyear's vulcanization process, a revolutionary technology of heat-bonding rubber to fabric that was far superior to the old-fashioned glue method.

Within a few years of their confederation, the constituent companies of U.S. Rubber were marketing rubber-soled shoes under a bewildering array of thirty different brand names, and by 1913 the need to agree on a single brand had become obvious.

The first choice for a brand name was the logical and catchy "Peds," from the Latin *ped*, meaning "foot." Unfortunately, Peds was already trademarked by one of the few companies *not* part of U.S. Rubber, so management apparently then sang a few rounds of "The Name Game" (Pedda pedda bo fedda, fee fy mo fedda . . .), trying out new initial consonants. After exhausting all twenty-five permutations of Peds, two candidates remained by 1916: Veds and Keds. The choice between the wispy and vaguely creepy "Veds" and the hard-consonant all-American "Keds" was a no-brainer, and soon kids were skinning their knees in Keds sneakers all over America. More fashionable and fancier rubber-soled shoes may have grabbed the spotlight since then, but Keds, now manufactured by the Stride Rite Corporation, keep ticking along.

Levi's

If Levi Strauss had stayed home, chances are we'd all be wearing corduroy and that *whoosh-whoosh* noise would have driven us mad years ago.

Fortunately, the inventor of modern blue jeans, born Loeb Strauss in Bavaria in 1829, was never a man to sit still. Along with his mother and two sisters, Strauss sailed for the New World in 1847 and quickly went to work in his half brothers' dry goods business in New York City.

Within a few years, Loeb had changed his first name to Levi, become an American citizen, and set out for San Francisco to bring the family dry goods business to the West Coast, then blossoming as a market in the heady days of the Gold Rush.

For the next twenty years, Levi Strauss sold blankets, pillows, clothing, and the like all over the West, and gained a reputation for honest goods and business practices. Much of the work clothing he sold was made of denim (from serge de Nîmes, serge cloth from the town of Nîmes, in France), a rugged and durable cotton fabric popular among miners. (Denim pants were also known as jeans, due to a bit of popular confusion with "jean" cloth, a less durable cotton/wool blend named for Genoa, Italy.)

In 1872, Strauss received a letter from a Nevada tailor named Jacob Davis, who explained that he had come up with a way to strengthen the only weak points found in the denim pants he made. By adding metal rivets at stress points, such as pocket corners, Davis had eliminated the eventual annoying tears, and his customers were ecstatic. Davis wanted to patent his invention, but lacked the funds, and proposed a business partnership with Strauss.

Strauss agreed, and with the new invention and his marketing skills built the business that more than any other convinced Americans to adopt blue jeans as their national uniform.

Manolo Blahnik

They are, it is said, to die for. Or at least to skip meals for a month (or maybe two) for. And heaven help the poor sap who refers to them as "just shoes."

Manolo Blahniks are probably the most famous, arguably the most expensive (average price $1,000 a pair), and certainly the most coveted (only a few of each style are made every year) women's shoes in the world.

Oddly enough, Manolo Blahnik himself did not set out to become a cult designer. Born in 1943 in the Canary Islands,

Blahnik first studied law and politics at the University of Geneva but then changed paths in 1968 and moved to Paris, where he considered becoming a theatrical designer. Over the next few years, Blahnik traveled, designing furniture and clothing, and making well-connected friends. One such friend, Paloma Picasso, introduced Blahnik to legendary *Vogue* editor Diana Vreeland. Blahnik, Vreeland declared, was wasting his talents on scenery and furniture—he should be designing shoes. "So I did it," said Blahnik. "And then I got hooked." By the mid-1970s, increasing numbers of the fashion elite were finding themselves hooked on Blahnik's creations, and in 1998 HBO's hit series *Sex and the City* introduced Manolo Blahnik shoes to the entire United States.

Nike

Although Phil Knight, as CEO, president, and chairman of the board, is the highly visible public face of Nike, Inc., he never would have gotten past the starting line without Bill Bowerman. Bowerman, legendary track coach at the University of Oregon, was the man primarily responsible for popularizing both track and field competition and jogging in postwar America. But in 1958, Bowerman was dissatisfied with the primitive design of American running shoes, clumsy cousins of the German Adidas brand that then dominated the sport. Along with Knight, a former runner under his tutelage, Bowerman formed Blue Ribbon Sports and began to import Tiger brand running shoes from Japan.

But from the beginning, Bowerman had been determined to design and make his own running shoes, and in 1971 he and Knight stopped dealing with Tiger and relaunched their operation as an independent manufacturing company. Pressed to come up with a new name, Knight had all forty-five company employees at the time toss their suggestions into a hat and picked one. The winner was "Nike," the winged Greek goddess of victory. Knight's own suggestion had been "Dimension Four."

While the image of winged victory was certainly appropriate for a running shoe company, a simpler logo than that of a Greek goddess was needed for the shoes and their packaging. With the deadline for an important presentation looming, Knight approached a young freelance designer, Carolyn Davidson, and asked her to design a logo for Nike. She came up with the company name superimposed over a stylized swoosh suggesting motion, and although Knight wasn't crazy about the design at first ("I don't love it, but it will grow on me," he said), he paid Davidson $35 and sent the design to the printers.

Within a few years, of course, the Nike name and Davidson's $35 swoosh became two of the most well known trademarks on the planet. Davidson, incidentally, eventually made out quite a bit better than that $35. In 1988, Knight invited her to lunch, where he surprised her with a gold "swoosh" ring and a hefty chunk of Nike stock.

Playtex

Playtex, which for much of its history has seemed a rather risqué name (at least to schoolboys) for an underwear company, evidently had a completely innocent origin. The company, established in Rochester, New York, in 1932, initially was called the International Latex Corporation (ILC), and for the first decade of its existence sold latex bathing caps and swimwear. The name Playtex may have been developed for use in marketing latex clothing for toddlers. From there the company moved on to manufacturing girdles (which were first sold as reducing devices) and other underwear. Eventually, ILC changed its corporate name to Playtex, and in 1975 renamed itself Playtex International.

The Gods Must Be Incorporated

There may be nothing new under the sun, but many consumers would be surprised to learn that the names of some of their favorite products hark back to ancient times and, in particular, to characters from Greek and Roman mythology. The lure of naming a product after a god or mythological figure is obvious: such a name confers instant classiness (although naming a muffler company after King Midas might seem like a bit of a stretch), it associates your product with the virtues of the mythological character (at least among classics majors), and, unless a very similar product has already snatched up the name, it can be easily trademarked. Olympus running shoes, for instance, would probably get no grief from the camera company of the same name. Conversely, once a name has been associated with a particular product, it may be considered a bit tainted by that use, which is probably why there's no soft drink named Trojan.

Occasionally the use of a mythological name is once-removed from its source, usually because the name has first become the personal or family name of the company's founder, etc., or has become familiar in another context, e.g., the Amazon River.

Here are some modern brands with names that evoke the days when gods roamed the earth:

Ajax—A heroic Greek warrior famed for his courage in the Trojan War (see Trojan, below). Brave Ajax is now primarily known as the name of a popular kitchen and bathroom cleanser.

Amazon—In Greek mythology, a race of women warriors known for their fierceness in battle. In South America, a very long river. Today the name of the leading online bookseller, said to have been chosen by founder Jeff Bezos because he wanted the store's inventory to be as deep and as wide as the Amazon River.

Eos—The Greek goddess of the dawn, known to the Romans as Aurora. Today the name of a line of cameras manufactured by Canon.

Hermes—The Greek name for Mercury (see below). Best known today as a maker of high-priced scarves and handbags, named after its founder Thierry Hermès.

Janus—Roman god of vigilance and wisdom, making him a logical choice for the high-profile investment company Janus International, although investors with a knowledge of mythology may remember that Janus is usually depicted as having two faces.

Mars—The Roman god of war, known to the Greeks as Ares. A leading maker of candy bars (Milky Way, Snickers, etc.), Mars, Inc. actually takes its name from its founder, Franklin Mars.

Mercury—Messenger of the gods in Roman mythology, fleet of foot and usually portrayed wearing winged sandals and helmet. Known primarily as the venerable make of automobile (a brand of the Ford Motor Company), although a graphic rendition of Mercury is used as the symbol of FTD florists.

Midas—King of Phrygia who, given one wish by the gods, chose the power to turn anything to gold with his touch. Midas quickly discovered that his "Midas touch" made eating and drinking impossible, so he begged to have it removed. Generally associated with wealth and good fortune, Midas is now the name of a leading automotive muffler company.

Olympus—Mount Olympus, in Greece, was thought by the ancients to be the home of the gods, making *Olympian* a synonym for "exalted" or "majestic." Olympus Group is a maker of cameras and imaging systems.

Oracle—A seer or psychic, a mortal who conveyed messages from the gods. A fitting choice for Oracle Corporation, manufacturers of database software. Something about mythology seems to attract software companies. The most famous of the ancient seers was the oracle at Delphi, in

Greece, and today Delphi lives on as the name of a popular programming language developed by Borland Software Corporation.

Orion—In Greek mythology, a renowned hunter who was slain by the goddess Artemis and became a constellation. Today most recognized as the name of a motion picture company.

Saturn—Roman god of the harvest and agriculture. Presumably the Saturn brand of cars owned by General Motors was named after the planet Saturn to convey an "otherworldly" automotive experience.

Thunderbird—A mythical giant bird renowned in Native American religions, believed to cause thunder and winds with the beating of its enormous wings. Known today as both a brand of Ford automobile and an inexpensive wine.

Trojan—An inhabitant of the city-state of Troy, which waged a bitter ten-year battle with Greece. The Trojans lost the war only because they fell for the Trojan horse, a trick gift from the Greeks. *Trojan* has long been synonymous with courage, strength, and perseverance. Presumably it was the "strength" aspect of the name that made it a good choice for a brand of condoms.

TECHNOLOGY, TOYS, AND ASSORTED BRIGHT IDEAS

Apple Computers, Macintosh

From little seeds mighty brands grow, but sometimes it's a bit hard to separate the fruit from the hokum.

The origin of the Apple name is the stuff of multiple legends, but the core story is simple. Steven Wozniak and Steven Jobs, Apple's founders, had been high school friends who had both gone on to work in Silicon Valley. Wozniak was especially interested in designing a new kind of computer, and when he eventually came up with what would become the Apple I, Jobs suggested that they try to market the machine. Needing a name for their partnership, the pair settled on Apple for several reasons: (1) Jobs had once spent a summer working on an apple farm and considered apples the perfect fruit; (2) Jobs also was a big Beatles fan and admired the group's Apple Corps. label and marketing firm; and (3) they were in a hurry to get started and neither Jobs nor Wozniak could think of a better name.

On April 1, 1976, Apple Computer was launched. As a tribute to the Beatles, the name must be counted as a mixed success, since Apple Computer has, since its founding, been sued three times by the Beatles' Apple Corps. for trademark infringement.

The next step was to come up with a logo. A friend named Ron Wayne created the first version, featuring Isaac Newton sitting under an apple tree to convey a sense of innovative inspiration. For his help, Jobs and Wozniak gave Wayne 10 percent of the company. But Jobs didn't really like the logo, considering it too cluttered, and soon pressed for adopting a simple apple silhouette. Unfortunately, according to Jobs, the result looked more like an orange than an apple, so the distinctive bite from the side of the fruit was added and the famous Apple logo was born.

The Macintosh computer line, introduced by Apple in 1984, takes its name from the popular apple variety, which in turn harks back to the Scottish surname MacIntosh, which means "son of the chieftain." Apparently Jobs actually wanted to call the machine the "Apple Bicycle," and even after his suggestion was rejected, he stubbornly made a point of referring to the Mac as "a bicycle for the mind."

Barbie

Call her the preternaturally perky perennial preteen product with a past.

Don't tell the millions of Barbie devotees who have made Mattel's doll a billion-selling global sensation since 1959, but Barbie's original name wasn't Barbie—it was the far more staid "Barbara." Ruth Handler, who founded Mattel in 1945 with her husband and another investor, named the doll after her own daughter.

Handler's inspiration was, however, the realization that young girls didn't really want to play with baby dolls. They wanted grown-up figures upon which they could project their dreams of love and romance. Handler developed and marketed the first adult woman doll and revolutionized the toy industry. Today three Barbie dolls are sold every second somewhere in the world.

Of course, Barbie isn't exactly a normal adult woman, and her unlikely physical proportions reflect a lineage Mattel would rather forget. Handler modeled the doll on a German gag gift for men, a toy derived from a risqué comic strip character named Lilli, a practitioner of the world's oldest profession. Barbie is, to put it bluntly, a recycled German hooker.

No wonder her boyfriend Ken (created in 1961 and named after Handler's son) always looked a bit anxious. Sadly (at least for Ken), Mattel announced just before Valentine's Day 2004 that Barbie and Ken were breaking up after forty-three years of going steady. Russell Arons, vice president of marketing at Mattel, explained that the pair "feel it's time to spend some quality time—apart," and denied rumors that the split was caused by the arrival of a new male doll, Blaine, described as "an Australian boogie boarder."

Barnes & Noble

Barnes & Noble, although it has been blamed by some for driving independent booksellers from the field, is actually the progeny of two very dedicated bibliophiles.

Way back in 1873, Charles M. Barnes started a book-selling business out of his home in Wheaton, Illinois. Barnes apparently passed his love of books to his son, who in 1917 traveled to New York City, where he met G. Clifford Noble. Together they opened a small bookstore in the city, and a few years later expanded into what would become their flagship store at Fifth Avenue and Eighteenth Street.

Barnes & Noble chugged happily along for the next few decades but fell on hard times in the late 1960s, the beginning of a period that saw the extinction of dozens of independent bookstores in New York City. Fortunately, Barnes & Noble caught the eye of Leonard Riggio, a successful college bookstore owner, who bought the chain in 1971 and set out on a course of expansion that eventually would spawn more than six hundred Barnes & Noble stores and a successful online presence, as well as almost two hundred B. Dalton and Doubleday bookshops.

BIC

It's a good thing that Marcel Bich wasn't fixated on his own name, otherwise one of the most famous advertising slogans of the 1970s would have been "Flick Your Bich."

In 1945, Bich, having been production manager for a French ink manufacturer, bought a factory near Paris and began making parts for fountain pens and mechanical pencils. As a pen professional, Bich recognized that the ballpoint pen, then a novelty in postwar Europe, was the wave of the writing future, and by 1950, Bich and his partner, Edouard Buffard, were marketing their own ballpoints in Europe. But Bich realized that his own name might be hard for non-French buyers to pronounce correctly, so he shortened it to simply "BIC," and within a few short years the world was inundated with inexpensive, stylish, and wildly popular BIC pens. In 1973 BIC branched out into plastic butane lighters (making the slogan "Flick your BIC" a worldwide double entendre), and a few years later BIC pioneered the disposable plastic shaving razor. Today BIC markets a wide range of writing, shaving, and office products as well as plastic sailboards.

The BIC logo, incidentally, features a character known as the BIC Boy, a schoolboy with the head of a ballpoint, designed in 1961 by legendary French graphic designer Raymond Savignac.

BIC isn't the only family name associated with ballpoint pens. In the U.K., ballpoints are commonly known as biros, after Ladislas and Georg Biro, the Hungarian brothers who developed and marketed the first practical ballpoint pens during World War II.

Borders

It sounds like a good name for a Tex-Mex restaurant, but Borders is, of course, a national chain of bookstores and Barnes & Noble's chief competitor.

Borders was founded in 1971 when Tom and Louis Borders, brothers living in Ann Arbor, Michigan, started a small used book shop. Early on, the brothers Borders instituted an inventory control system that, when they opened several more stores, allowed them to customize each store's offerings to the tastes of the surrounding community. Today there are more than 450 Borders superstores across the United States, but only half the inventory in any store is standard to the chain. The rest is stocked to match the store's clientele.

In 1994, Borders was acquired by Kmart, which also bought Waldenbooks, a chain of mall bookstores founded in 1933 in Bridgeport, Connecticut (and named after Henry David Thoreau's classic, *Walden*). But just a year later Borders bought itself and Waldenbooks back from Kmart and now operates both chains.

Brawny

The hard part of creating a brand is usually identifying your market and thinking up the name. From there on out it's just a matter of spelling stuff right in your ads and hoping your product isn't cited by the FDA as a source of skin rashes and insanity. But then there are the high-maintenance cases.

Brawny (meaning "strong, muscular") comes from *brawn*, meaning "strength." It's a good name for a cleaning product (notwithstanding that the root of *brawn* is an Old French word meaning "hindquarters of an animal suitable for roasting").

So when Georgia-Pacific introduced Brawny brand paper towels in 1974, it must have seemed a stroke of genius to personify the name Brawny with an illustration of a brawny man on the package. Sort of a Mr. Clean with hair (and sans earring), Brawny Man was ostensibly a lumberjack (carrying a peavey, a type of logging tool, on his shoulder) but also definitely a '70s guy. Clad in a red plaid shirt, Brawny Man sported a longish shag hairdo and a neatly trimmed mustache, looking more than a little like a lost member of the Village People.

By 1984 fashions had changed, and Brawny Man got his first haircut, a shorter version of the original but still parted in the center. His eye color switched, for no apparent reason, from brown to green. By 1991, the hair was starting to look a bit weird, so Brawny Man switched to a side part. In 2000, he finally ditched the plaid shirt in favor of denim.

But apparently there's only so much makeover you can swing with a thirty-year-old lumberjack, because in 2003 Brawny Man disappeared entirely, replaced by a Stepford Brawny Clone with short dark hair, more visible biceps, and the cocky demeanor of a stockbroker on steroids.

Canon

Now known as a global corporation producing a vast array of business and data management systems as well as cameras, Canon has succeeded beyond its founders' wildest dreams. But even in the early days, Canon understood the need for a name that would have international appeal.

Canon began as the Precision Optical Instruments Laboratory in Tokyo, a project set up in 1933 by a passionate camera bug named Goro Yoshida and his brother-in-law, Saburo Uchida, with financing supplied by their friend Takeshi Mitarai. Yoshida's ambition was to make a 35 millimeter camera in Japan that could compete with the great German brands,

Leica and Contax, that then dominated the photography market.

By 1934, Yoshida's factory was producing Japan's first high-end 35mm camera, a Leica clone that Yoshida, a Buddhist, named Kwanon after the Buddhist goddess of mercy. More sophisticated cameras followed in the next few years, and eventually Yoshida's creations attained the serious reputation among professional photographers that he had dreamed of.

But soon after the first Kwanon camera hit the market, Yoshida's partner Uchida raised a question about the name. A camera brand named for a Buddhist deity seemed old-fashioned and stuffy, not a good choice for what should be seen as a precision high-tech company. Together, the partners decided to rename their brand Canon, with its invocation of unwavering standards and precision. Best of all, the pronunciation of Canon was so close to Kwanon that potential customers who had heard of their camera would not be confused by the name change. So Kwanon officially became Canon in 1935, even adopting the distinctive logo still used today.

Chia Pets

It only seems as if Chia Pets have been around forever. The clay figurines sold with seeds that eventually grow into luxuriant "hair" were actually first invented and marketed by Joseph Enterprises, Inc. of San Francisco in 1977.

Chia Pets take their name from the chia plant seeds that

come with the figurines. Chia (*Salvia columbariae*) is actually a member of the sage family, and if you were to plant the seeds outdoors and wait a few months, you'd have a perfectly edible harvest. Mixed with water into a paste spread over the figurine, however, chia sprouts haven't the room to grow roots and flourish.

Chia Pets today come in a wide variety of shapes, from Chia Kitten and Chia Hippo to Chia Heads and even a Chia Elmer Fudd, and can provide months of enjoyment for people who derive enjoyment from things that just sit there and grow slowly. Firsthand research by the author has, however, firmly established that a Chia Tweety Bird is not considered an appropriate anniversary gift for a spouse.

Day-Glo

Contrary to what the guy at your local head shop may have told you, Day-Glo colors were not invented by Jimi Hendrix, although they were, predictably, dreamed up in California.

Brothers Bob and Joe Switzer developed the first "daylight fluorescent" pigments back in the 1930s. The secret of such pigments lies in absorbing light of various wavelengths and reemitting it as one specific color, thus appearing far brighter than normal colors under any lighting. In the early days, the Switzers' pigments were used primarily on movie and magic show posters, and in 1936 the Switzers went to work for a Cleveland, Ohio, firm producing movie posters. During

World War II, the Switzers produced high-visibility signal panels for the Army, a technology that proved profitable for Switzer Bros., Inc. in the postwar billboard boom.

As the use of their pigments expanded into advertising and marketing, the Switzers trademarked them as "DayGlo" colors, highlighting their "glowing" appearance even in normal daylight. Oddly enough, it wasn't until the late 1960s, when posters made with Day-Glo pigments were most often seen under ultraviolet, or black, light, that Switzer Bros., Inc. finally got around to changing its corporate name to Day-Glo Color Corporation. Today Day-Glo fluorescent products are used in graphics, paint, and packaging, and studies have shown that Day-Glo colors are noticed 75 percent faster than standard colors (and probably even faster if Jimi Hendrix music is present).

Dolby

"Trust the . . . HISS . . . Force, . . . POP . . . HUM . . . Luke." If that doesn't match your memories of *Star Wars,* you have Ray Dolby to thank.

While still an engineering undergraduate at Stanford University, Dolby worked on the team at Ampex Corporation that perfected the first video recorder. After his return in 1965 from a stint in India as a U.N. adviser, Dolby established Dolby Laboratories to explore his ideas for removing the hiss and other noise that then plagued most tape recordings. Dolby's insight was to separate the good sound from the bad noise by filtering the output of the tape into separate audio channels, allowing the noise to be removed without muffling the remaining sound as all then-existing techniques did. Once Dolby had perfected his multitracking technology, it revolutionized both the studio recording industry and the home tape player market, hastening the demise of the long-playing record.

In 1975, Dolby Labs introduced a similar revolutionary technique for quieting the noise on film sound tracks, and George Lucas was one of the first directors to put the new tools to use in his film *Star Wars,* the success of which Lucas partially credits to his Dolby-enhanced sound track. Dolby systems are now employed in nearly all movie theaters.

eBay

If Pierre Omidyar had been a little quicker on his feet, the name eBay would be nothing but an annoying typo today.

In 1995, Omidyar, a French-Iranian immigrant and Silicon Valley veteran, created a Web site he called Auction Web, an electronic flea market where visitors could hawk Beanie Babies, computer gear, and the Pez dispensers his then girlfriend (now wife) collected. Unfortunately, the Internet gold rush was by then in full swing, and the domain name auctionweb.com was already taken, as was echobay.com (after Omidyar's Echo Bay Technology Group). But ebay.com was ripe for the picking, and Omidyar snapped it up. And from that third-choice domain name, the Internet's premier auction site grew. Today on a typical day there are more than 16 million items up for auction on eBay in more than 16,000 categories, and in 2002 eBay members unloaded more than $14 billion worth of goods on the site. Presumably, Mrs. Omidyar now rarely gets outbid on Pez dispensers.

Since domain names on the Internet do not distinguish between upper- and lowercase letters, the distinctive capitalization "eBay" was not, strictly speaking, necessary. But the alternative "ebay" would most likely have usually been pronounced "eh-bay" or "eb-ay," more evocative of a startled diner ("Eb-AY! That's hot!") than a multibillion-dollar business empire. The lowercase *e-* prefix also evokes the great '90s e-commerce boom, a boom of whose fizzle eBay is probably the most wildly successful survivor.

Eureka

There was a time when most schoolchildren in America would have been able to explain why Eureka vacuum cleaners bear that name.

The origin of Eureka lies in ancient Greece, where, according to legend, a certain king of Syracuse commissioned a goldsmith to fashion a new crown for him. The king suspected that the artisan had substituted cheaper silver, and turned to the philosopher Archimedes for a way to prove his case. While mulling the problem over, Archimedes decided to take a bath. Getting into his bath, he noticed that the water rose as he sat down, and realized that gold, being denser than silver, would displace less water than silver, and that the honesty of the

King's goldsmith could be measured by just such a simple test. When Archimedes realized this, goes the story, he leaped from the bathtub and ran through the streets of Syracuse stark naked shouting *"Eureka! Eureka!,"* which is Greek for "I have found it!"

Fast-forward now to Detroit in 1909, where businessman Fred Wardell was founding his company to produce a new lightweight kind of vacuum cleaner. Wardell felt that Eureka was the perfect name for his creation, because he believed that his new lightweight design would revolutionize housecleaning. Within a few years the industry apparently agreed, awarding Eureka the Grand Prize at the 1915 San Francisco International Exposition. And Fred Wardell didn't even have to get in a bathtub.

Exxon

The 1980s and '90s saw a flurry of corporate renamings, with companies once considered household words choosing, for reasons that ranged from cross-industry mergers to what seemed like sheer perversity, to change their spots. In some cases, the apparent motive was a desire to project a more modern, "synergistic" image less tied to specific products. Thus the venerable International Harvester, redolent of cornfields and tractors, became Navistar, and U.S. Steel ducked into a phone booth and came out wearing a somewhat cryptic USX cape and tights.

The mother of all modern corporate moniker swapping,

however, had come a decade earlier, in 1972, when Standard Oil of New Jersey, better known to the public as Esso since 1926, decided to change its name. Esso itself had been a fairly clever name in its day, a playful phonetic rendition of Standard Oil.

It took Esso three years to pick a new name, during which the company reportedly spent more than $100 million and pored over at least ten thousand possibilities. As has become standard practice in such renaming campaigns, the criteria were that the new name be short, easy to pronounce, and impossible to misspell; that it preferably mean nothing in English; and that it have no unpleasant connotations or unfortunate meanings in another language.

And the winner was, to considerable public incredulity, Exxon. If the Esso team had been searching for novelty, they had certainly found it—no word extant in the English language contains the double *x* form. And if they were looking for publicity, they had found bushels of that, too, much of it negative. Language mavens were outraged at the artificiality and unorthodox form of Exxon, and declared the new name an offense against the English language. Some Exxon stockholders loudly questioned why such an ugly new name had cost so much money.

Eventually, of course, consumers got used to the new Exxon, but the company found itself facing another PR hurdle in 1989, when its supertanker *Exxon Valdez* ruptured and spilled almost 11 million gallons of oil into Alaska's Prince William Sound, polluting hundreds of miles of coastline and killing wildlife. The name Exxon instantly became associated in the public mind with oil-covered seabirds. The company could only sweat out the scandal, but for the ship itself, once repairs had been done, a bit of renaming was in order. So the company rechristened the *Exxon Valdez* the *Sea River Mediterranean*, a name which, as the BBC put it at the time, ". . . is more likely to conjure up visions of long balmy holiday evenings than a horrendous oil slick." The company also promised that the newly rehabilitated ship would live out its days in the Mediterranean and never, ever, sail anywhere near Alaska again.

FedEx

One thing's for sure: Frederick W. Smith didn't copy his Yale undergraduate term paper off the Internet. Of course, there wasn't an Internet back in 1965, but Smith would never have done so anyway, because apart from being honest, he had a point to make in his paper. The way airfreight shippers did business at that time was all wrong, Smith wrote. Their antiquated routing system might work for truck deliveries that were expected to take a week or more but were utterly inadequate for air shipments that ought to be delivered within a day or two.

By 1971, Smith was operating his own small airfreight company and doing serious thinking about how to organize a national air transport network. By 1973, Smith's Federal Express was delivering packages all over the eastern United States from its hub in Memphis, Tennessee, picked for its central location and generally good weather.

Smith had picked the name Federal Express for its connotation of national financial activity, and in fact had, at the outset, hoped to snag a contract with the Federal Reserve Bank that unfortunately failed to materialize. But within a few years Federal Express was the unchallenged leader in high-speed air delivery and was growing at about 40 percent per year.

By the early 1990s, Federal Express had realized that its customers rarely actually used the name Federal Express; they would speak of sending a package by "Fed Ex" or even use "Fedex" as a verb. So in 1994, Federal Express officially changed its corporate name to FedEx. In 2000, the overnight air delivery service was named FedEx Express to differentiate it from other FedEx divisions such as FedEx Ground (formerly Roadway Package System).

Fender

"Thank God," said Keith Richards when the Rolling Stones were being inducted into the Rock and Roll Hall of Fame in 1989, "for Leo Fender."

Richards's gratitude was well placed, for without Leo Fender, modern rock music would simply not exist. In 1948, Fender, a former radio repair shop owner, introduced the world's first solid-body electric guitar. Until that time, electric guitars had been more or less standard hollow-body acoustic instruments with a magnetic pickup added. But Fender's Broadcaster guitar (later renamed the Telecaster) was a purely electric creation with a new, clear sound. His subsequent

Stratocaster model, with its three pickups and tremolo bar, a favorite of guitar gods such as Eric Clapton and Jimi Hendrix, revolutionized the sound of popular music in the 1950s and '60s.

Formica

Devotees of TV home-renovation and decorating shows know that the really important decision in redoing the family kitchen today has nothing to do with appliances, lighting, or what you put on the floor. No, it's by your countertops that you shall be judged, and many's the home loan that has been floated to bridge the golden gap betwixt faux marble and the real, preferably imported Italian, article. Whether the subsequent bologna sandwiches taste better for being prepared on such a pricey surface is, of course, debatable.

Back in the 1950s and '60s, however, the fashionable modern home was one whose owners had sprung for the countertop of the future—Formica. By the late 1960s and through the '70s, in fact, Formica seemed to top nearly every flat surface in the land. Restaurant tables, school desks, retail counters, and even the floor of Radio City Music Hall in New York City were all made of sleek, smooth Formica.

For a biology student of the day, the name Formica must have presented a bit of a puzzle. Formica is also the genus name of the taxonomic family Formicidae, those pesky little insects better known as ants.

Fortunately, there is no connection between the name

Formica and ants, but the path Formica took from its invention to America's countertops was a bit convoluted. Way back in 1912, Dan J. O'Conor was a young engineer working for Westinghouse in Pittsburgh when he had a good idea. If you were to coat fabric with resin while it rolled onto a spindle, you could then cut the roll lengthwise, flatten it, and, after curing, you would have a laminate material that would be light, durable, and, most important to O'Conor's line of work, an excellent electrical insulator. O'Conor promptly took his invention to his bosses at Westinghouse, who agreed that it was a clever idea and paid him, according to standard company policy, the princely sum of one dollar for the patent.

Mr. O'Conor must have been less than thrilled with this treatment, because within weeks he and his friend Herbert A. Faber both quit Westinghouse and started their own company to produce insulators employing the same general resin laminate idea. At that time the standard material for electrical insulators was mica, a natural family of minerals. As the new synthetic material was intended as a *substitute for mica,* the name Formica was a natural.

The next few years were filled with legal skirmishes as Faber and O'Conor battled Westinghouse and other companies over patent issues. But Formica Corporation prevailed, and today is a world leader in laminate materials. Westinghouse, incidentally, makes everything from toasters to nuclear power plants today, but wisely has left the countertop market to Formica.

What Were They Thinking?

It all started, perhaps, with the Edsel, proudly introduced by the Ford Motor Company in 1957. The car's name was taken from that of Edsel Bryant Ford, former Ford president and Henry Ford's son, but it's hard to pin the ensuing debacle on Edsel himself because he had died back in 1943. There were two major problems with the Edsel, both of which became immediately apparent. First, it was a remarkably strange-looking car with a bizarre horse collar–shaped grille design that led one wag to compare the Edsel to "an Oldsmobile sucking a lemon."

Second, Edsel was an exceedingly weird name for a car, especially coming from Ford, home of such all-American models as the Thunderbird, Falcon, and Mustang. The strangeness of the name was made all the more mystifying by the fact that Ford had actually assembled a panel of three hundred outside consultants, including poet Marianne Moore, to come up with a name for their new car. Apparently Ford then discarded the panel's suggestions, because it is implausible that anyone of sound mind and not working for Ford could have suggested Edsel.

Public reaction to the Edsel ranged from helpless laughter to outright hostility, and the model was shelved after only three years. In fairness to the Edsel, it did introduce some advanced features for its time, such as self-adjusting brakes and a speedometer that glowed when a preset speed limit was exceeded, but Edsel today remains synonymous with "really bad product name."

Though Edsel may have been a bad choice for naming a car, it was at least a real name without bizarre connotations, which is more than can be said for some of the brand names of the past few years. Some bad names, such as Cruex, are simply the result of tone deafness to the implications or sound of the name. Others, especially those produced during the Internet boom of the 1990s or cooked up in a hurry to distance companies from the corporate scandals of the early twenty-first century, are mind-numbingly meaningless concoctions of almost-words often born, it seems, in the mechanical minds of computers.

It may be, as the naming consultants say, that all the good "real" names are already taken. But some of the examples noted below are enough to make one wonder if naming companies and products with simple personal names—"Bob" or "Louise," for instance, or maybe even "Edsel"—might be a better approach.

Achieva—A car from Oldsmobile, sounds like *achiever* spoken with a Brooklyn accent. Supposedly the model was originally going to be called the Achiever, but company execs felt that was a bit too blatant.

Agilent—It sounds like a maker of sporting equipment, but it's actually a communications company spun off from Hewlett-Packard. The problem with the name is that you're going to forget that fact in about thirty seconds.

Altria—Supposedly intended to invoke the Latin *alt*, meaning "high." Nice try, gang, but we'll just keep calling you guys Philip Morris.

Avaya—Another corporate spin-off, this time from Lucent Technologies. The company says its name suggests "agility, speed, and commitment," but isn't "Avaya!" what Desi Arnaz used to shout when he was upset?

Blonder Tongue—Maybe it's what you get if your mouth turns a whiter shade of pale. Blonder Tongue makes communications equipment, and the name really isn't their fault, since they were founded by Isaac (Ike) S. Blonder and Ben H. Tongue in 1950. Then again, that's plenty of time to think up a nondisgusting name, guys.

Boring Business Systems—An office systems company in Florida, founded in 1924 and still run by the Boring family. Family pride is good, but in this case it must have cost at least a few sales over the years.

Consignia—If it ain't broke, fix it until it is. In early 2001 the British Post Office announced that it was changing its name after three hundred years to coincide with its transformation into a semi-autonomous public corporation as part of the deregulation of the postal industry in the U.K. The new name, product of a two-year, million-pound search by the naming consultants Dragon Brands, was Consignia. As a representative of Dragon Brands cornered by the BBC later nervously explained, "It's got 'consign' in it. It's got a link with 'insignia,' so there is this kind of royalty-ish thing in the back of one's mind." But in the front of everyone else's mind, including that of Consignia's chairman, was an instant desire to deep-six the new name. After a brief tussle over the cost of ditching it, Consignia was history and folks were again mailing letters at the Royal Mail Post Office.

Cruex—An antifungal powder intended to be applied to the most sensitive areas of the human body. A cruex and unusual name for such a product.

Fifth Third Bancorp—Started out as the Bank of Ohio, but that was thirty-six mergers ago, and somebody finally just threw in the old naming towel.

Grand Vitara—An SUV produced by Suzuki. Sounds like either an extinct bird or a very serious intestinal disorder.

Incipient—Another dippy data company name. *Incipient*, of course, means "about to happen," as in "Finding your data is incipient, we promise."

McDATA—They make "data storage solutions." Does the Happy Megabyte Meal come with fries? Newsflash, McCoiners, "cute" and "reliable" do not go together.

Monday—In 2002, PwC Consulting, the unfortunately named consulting arm of the even-more-unfortunately named PricewaterhouseCoopers accounting firm, decided that it didn't like its name, which is understandable. What is harder to fathom is why they decided to rename their company after everyone's least-favorite day of the week—Monday. According to PwC CEO Greg Brenneman, "Our new name—Monday—is exactly what we want it to be as we create our new business: a real word, concise, recognizable, global, and the right fit for a company that works hard to deliver results."

The result PwC got was global derision, and it soon dropped the planned name change. Shortly thereafter, PwC was bought by IBM and everyone went back to making fun of Altria.

Poolife—A pool cleaning company that got carried away with the jam-the-name-together craze. As its Web site says, "Long lazy afternoons. The feel of the sun on your shoulders. That first refreshing plunge into the water. . . ." And you'd better call us because there's poo in there!

Zzyzx Peripherals, Inc.—They want you to know that it's pronounced "zee-zix." It's probably not a good idea to pick a name that makes anyone calling think their telephone is broken.

Frisbee

Poor William Russell Frisbie. When he moved to Bridgeport, Connecticut, to manage a new bakery in 1871, he never dreamed that someday half the dogs in America would be chasing his legacy across the nation's lawns.

Mr. Frisbie was a good baker. He was so good, in fact, that within a few years he had bought the bakery and established the Frisbie Pie Company, selling pies all across New England. Frisbie pies were especially popular among the students at Yale University, in New Haven, in the 1920s, and soon Yale dormitories were awash in empty Frisbie pie tins. College students being expert time-wasters, it wasn't long before the Yalies discovered that the Frisbie tins, if flung with a spinning motion, would waft gracefully through the air to be caught and returned by a fellow scholar. Since the tins were made of metal, however, it was advisable that the recipient know in advance that the pie tin had been launched, so the cry of "Frisbie!" was adopted as the game's equivalent of "Fore!" in golf.

Within a few years, the game of "Frisbie" had spread far beyond Yale. In 1948, a California building inspector and inventor named Fred Morrison began to manufacture and market the first flying disc made of plastic as the Frisbee, most likely modifying the spelling to avoid legal problems with the Frisbie Pie folks. In 1955, Morrison joined the Wham-O toy company, and in 1957 Wham-O began to market his disc as the Pluto Platter, neatly avoiding the trademark question entirely while also capitalizing on the national obsession with UFOs.

By 1958, however, the venerable Frisbie Pie Company had gone out of business, and Wham-O quickly renamed its disc the Frisbee and trademarked the name. Frisbeemania followed and continues to this day, and while Wham-O won't say exactly how many Frisbees are sold every year, they do slyly estimate that the number is probably greater than sales of footballs, baseballs and basketballs, combined.

Google

Back in the 1930s, U.S. mathematician Edward Kasner was trying to think of a name for a very, very large number, ten raised to the hundredth power, and decided to pose the question to his nine-year-old nephew, Milton Sirotta. Little Milton gave the matter some serious thought and after a few minutes came up with "googol." Uncle Edward knew a winner when he heard one, he popularized the term among his fellow mathematicians, and googol has ever since signified the numeral 1 followed by 100 zeroes.

There are two more interesting facts about googol. The word is something of a linguistic rarity, having been invented by an identifiable person and not being based on any other word. Evidently little Milton just dreamed it up out of thin air.

And while mathematicians, scientists, and exaggerators everywhere have found googol a useful name, don't go looking for one. There isn't a googol of anything in the known universe, not even a googol of atoms. That's how big a googol is.

Fast-forward now to 1996, when Larry Page and Sergey

Brin, who had met as graduate students at Stanford University, were perfecting their new method of searching the Internet. They had first dubbed their new search engine Back Rub because it, like Google today, worked by analyzing "back links" to a given Web site as an index of the site's credibility and reputation in the Net community. Page and Brin, having failed in their attempts to sell their technology to Silicon Valley, decided to create their own company.

Just why they abandoned the name Back Rub is not recorded in company press materials, but a fear of confusion with online massage parlors seems likely. Instead, when Brin and Page opened the doors of their new business in 1998, it was under the name Google. Today the company straightforwardly acknowledges Google as a variation of googol, reflecting "the company's mission to organize the immense, seemingly infinite amount of information available on the Web."

Though Brin and Page don't say so, they may have considered simply calling their invention Googol. If so, they soon discovered that they had missed the boat on that possibility. The googol.com domain had been registered by a Silicon Valley engineer named Tim Beauchamp back in 1995.

Hallmark

Joyce C. Hall was born in August 1891 in the small town of David City, Nebraska. Joyce was a boy, and his unusual first name bears explaining. Joyce's parents were deeply religious, and the lad happened to be born on the same day a Methodist bishop named Isaac W. Joyce paid David City a visit. (Bishops' visits apparently being an unusual occurrence in rural Nebraska, Joyce's two older brothers sported the more pedestrian names Rollie and William.)

When Joyce was sixteen, he and his brothers formed a company to sell imported postcards. The company didn't exactly fail, but it didn't really succeed either, and in 1910 Joyce dropped out of high school, packed all his postcards, and lit out for Kansas City. Within five years, Joyce and his brothers were back in business, running a gift and card shop in Kansas City. In 1915, however, a fire destroyed the shop, and instead of reopening, the Hall brothers bought an engraving firm, which they opened for business under the logical name of Hall Brothers Company. The Halls were now in the business of creating, not just selling, greeting cards.

Hall Brothers' business grew dramatically over the years, but Joyce Hall had never really liked the firm's name, arguing that "it sounded old-fashioned," and he pushed for changing their name to Hallmark. In fourteenth-century London, members of the goldsmiths' guild working at Goldsmiths' Hall had adopted a special symbol, known as a hall mark, to be stamped into their products to denote quality and authenticity. In general usage since that time, *hallmark* had come to mean "a mark placed or stamped on an article of trade to indicate its origin, purity, or genuineness." Joyce felt the term was perfect because it stood for the high quality the firm valued and also incorporated the Hall family name.

In 1928, Joyce finally managed to convince his brothers

and staff, and Hallmark Cards was born. Each card thereafter bore the legend "A Hallmark Card" on the back, along with the firm's redesigned symbol of a five-pointed crown. Joyce, it soon became apparent, had been right, and Hallmark Cards boomed. A few years later Hallmark became the first greeting card company to advertise on radio (and eventually TV), and with the addition of its signature slogan, "When You Care Enough to Send the Very Best," in 1944, became one of the most recognized brands on earth. The *Hallmark Hall of Fame*, originally created to market the company's cards, has showcased quality TV dramas for more than fifty years, earning seventy-eight Emmys since its 1951 debut. Not bad for a boy named Joyce.

Hoover

In 1907, Murray Spangler was an inventor in search of an invention. In the meantime, Murray was working nights as a janitor in a Canton, Ohio, department store. One night Murray was cleaning the carpets in the store using the preferred carpet-sweeping tool of the day—a broom. Murray noted that not only was sweeping carpets with a broom not exactly blazingly efficient, but the clouds of dust kicked up by his broom aggravated his asthma and made it very difficult to breathe.

Since Murray was an inventor, he sensed there had to be a better way, and he went home determined to find it. Using an old tin soap box, a fan, a broom handle, and a pillowcase, Murray fashioned a crude machine designed to suck up dust and deposit it in the pillowcase where it couldn't irritate his lungs. To Murray's mild amazement, the awkward gizmo actually worked, and he quickly set out to find a backer who would underwrite further development of his "suction sweeper," as he called it.

Fortunately, Murray had a cousin, Susan Hoover, who tried the machine, liked it, and promptly told her husband about it. Her husband, W. H. Hoover, owned a leather goods shop but was looking to diversify, and in Murray's new machine he saw a golden opportunity. Hoover bought the rights to Spangler's invention in 1908, kept Murray on as his partner, and began to develop and promote the machine through clever advertising and sales techniques.

Constant technological improvements and innovative marketing soon made Hoover a household word and market leader. Murray Spangler presumably made out all right too, although his name became just a footnote to Hoover history. Ironically, poor Murray's obscurity became even more striking in England, where to this day sweeping with a vacuum cleaner is popularly called "hoovering."

IKEA

It's like *The Little Match Girl* but with a happy ending. In Hans Christian Andersen's famous fable, a poor urchin perishes after being sent out on the frozen city streets to sell matches. But in the IKEA story, an enterprising farm boy builds match selling into a global empire.

Born in 1926 in the Swedish village of Agunnaryd, young Ingvar Kamprad got his start in business by riding his bicycle from farm to farm selling wooden matches to his neighbors. Once everyone had a supply of matches, Ingvar wisely decided to diversify his offerings, and soon was pedaling around the countryside delivering Christmas tree ornaments, ballpoint pens, and, though it must have been a bit awkward, fresh fish. By age seventeen, Ingvar had formed his own company and named it IKEA, an acronym made up of his own initials, the name of his family's farm (Elmtaryd), and the village of his birth, Agunnaryd.

Delivering his product line (which now included picture frames, watches, and jewelry) by bicycle was no longer practical, so Ingvar transformed IKEA into a mail-order operation and by 1948 was also selling furniture produced by local artisans. So successful was his low-priced but sturdy line of furniture that by 1951 Ingvar had dropped all his other products and decided to concentrate on inexpensive but stylish home furnishings. IKEA today operates stores in more than thirty countries around the world, selling about twelve thousand different products (but not, oddly enough, bicycles).

Jacuzzi

Candido Jacuzzi's first product was about as far from the relaxing water massage device that bears his name today as it is possible to imagine.

Jacuzzi's family immigrated to the United States from his birthplace of Casarza della Delizia, Italy, in the early twentieth century, settling in Berkeley, California. Together with his six brothers, Jacuzzi designed first propellers, then entire airplanes, during World War I, until a test flight gone awry killed one of his brothers and the Jacuzzis quit the field. He then put his knowledge of aerodynamic principles to use designing hydraulic pumps, and when his fifteen-month-old son developed severe arthritis in 1943, Jacuzzi designed a small jet pump that would transform a simple bath into a soothing massage. By the 1960s, Jacuzzi Brothers was marketing the first whirlpool tubs with integrated jet pumps, and by the 1970s America had gone hot tub crazy, making Jacuzzi a household synonym for the Good Life.

Kleenex

Although Kleenex, the world's leading facial tissue, is today used primarily as a disposable handkerchief, it was originally designed and marketed to help women remove cold cream from their faces—hence the "Kleen" element of the product's name.

The -*ex* suffix, connoting "out" or "away," was already popular among manufacturers of cleansing products when Kleenex was invented in 1924. But the International Cellucotton Products Company of Wisconsin had a more specific motivation in picking the name. Its flagship product at that time was Kotex feminine hygiene pads, and by grafting the *-ex* of Kotex onto *Kleen,* it took the first step toward establishing an easily identifiable family of products. The name Kotex, incidentally, had been invented to fuse the words *cotton texture* into one easy-to-remember name.

Although Kleenex had originally been marketed as a cleansing aid, by 1930 its manufacturers realized that Kleenex were catching more sneezes than cold cream and that they had, in effect, invented an entirely new category of product—facial tissues. In 1930 Kleenex changed its name to Kleenex Facial Tissue and today is made by Kimberly-Clark.

Kodak

Born in 1854 on a farm in upstate New York, George Eastman did not have a happy childhood. His father died when Eastman was just eight, and he had to leave school after seventh grade to seek work. But Eastman was resilient, energetic, and intellectually curious, and by age twenty-one he had a good job at a Rochester, New York, bank and was developing an interest in photography.

Photography at that time was undergoing a revolution, leaving behind the messy and cumbersome use of wet glass plates to make pictures and moving toward a more convenient, durable medium. In 1880, Eastman started a company to manufacture dry glass plates, and a year later resigned from his bank job to pursue photographic innovation full-time.

Two years later, Eastman unveiled his bombshell invention,

the Kodak camera photographic roll film that allowed customers to make multiple pictures without reloading their cameras.

In choosing "Kodak" for his camera and film, Eastman demonstrated a methodical approach to brand naming ahead of his time. The name must be short, Eastman decided, and impossible to misspell. Eastman liked the letter *K* for its forceful sound, so he spent some time mulling over as many possible short combinations beginning with that letter as he could come up with. He finally picked Kodak at least in part because it meant absolutely nothing and thus would be easy to defend as a trademark.

In 1888, Eastman debuted the Kodak camera, sold preloaded with enough film to take one hundred pictures. When the film was used up, the customer simply returned the camera to Eastman's company along with $10, and received in return prints and the camera reloaded with fresh film. George Eastman had simultaneously invented mass-market photography and the photofinishing industry in one fell swoop.

LEGO

According to the LEGO Web site, "On average every person on planet Earth has 52 LEGO bricks." Aside from being a good illustration of the statistical slipperiness of the word *average* (many of us own no LEGO bricks whatsoever that we know of), that statement (along with "327 billion LEGO elements have been molded since 1949") indicates that LEGO is one very hot toy company.

Although LEGO bricks are one of the world's most successful uses of plastics, the company's roots lie back in 1932 in the little town of Billund, Denmark, where plastics were probably very rare if not entirely unknown. In that year Ole Kirk Christiansen, a master carpenter, established a business manufacturing stepladders, ironing boards, stools, and, presumably as a sideline, wooden toys. By 1934, however, toys had become a big enough part of the business that Ole renamed his business LEGO, from the Danish words *leg godt,* meaning "play well." A bit further on, he discovered that *lego* is, serendipitously, also Latin for "I put together."

LEGO prospered and expanded over the following years, concentrating primarily on wooden toys such as the classic LEGO duck, and by 1949 had begun producing plastic Automatic Binding Bricks, the forerunner of today's LEGO bricks. Oddly enough, at the 1955 international debut of LEGO bricks at a toy fair in Nuremberg, Germany, the reaction from those present was not positive. Undeterred, LEGO soldiered on, spewing out bricks and a wide variety of other toys on its march to each of us owning those average fifty-two bricks.

So ubiquitous have LEGO sets become that if one could wrest just the ones sold in the past ten years from the hands of their little owners and place them end to end, the assembly would stretch from London to Perth. To any parent whose living room has been transformed into a LEGO minefield, this vision brings to mind a more literal translation of that Latin *lego,* namely "to pick up, to gather together scattered objects."

Famous Long Ago

Thinking up the perfect name for your business or product won't do you a bit of good if you can't hang onto it. The nightmare haunting every trademark holder is "genericization"—the transformation of a registered brand name, possibly the key to a company's fortune, into a simple common noun owned by nobody and available to any competitor.

In the United States, trademark protection can be lost for a variety of reasons buried in America's notoriously arcane trademark laws, but the most common cause is a failure to vigorously defend the trademarked name against use as a generic term for the entire class of products. Thus Xerox Corporation has for many years taken out ads imploring customers (with little success) not to use *xerox* as a casual synonym for "photocopy." The same concern is also the motive behind the stilted adjective-noun form (e.g., "Jell-O gelatin dessert") and fetishistic use of *brand* ("Jell-O brand pudding") often found in advertisements. Use of the product name alone, even by its manufacturer, opens the door to loss of the trademark.

Probably the most famous case of a name that was once trademarked but has long been used as a generic term is that of "aspirin," registered as a trademark for the analgesic acetylsalicylic acid by the German firm of Bayer AG in 1899. Bayer lost its trademark in most of the world after Germany lost World War I, and Sterling Drug registered Aspirin as its own trademark in the United States in 1918 (Bayer's patent on the formula of the drug itself had expired in 1917). But Sterling soon discovered (as Bayer had known for years) that there was no way to stop "aspirin" from being widely used as a generic term, and in 1921 it lost trademark protection of "aspirin" in the U.S. Interestingly, in Canada, Aspirin is still a trademarked name owned by Bayer.

Other terms that were once the pride and joy of clever coiners but are now up for grabs include:

Allen wrench—The little hexagonal screwdriver often included in "some assembly required" furniture kits. Originally a trademarked invention of the Allen Manufacturing Company in Hartford, Connecticut, and still usually capitalized.

Cellophane—Thin, transparent film, technically a type of paper as it is made from cellulose, invented in 1908 by Jacques Brandenberger, a Swiss textile engineer who was trying to develop a stainproof tablecloth.

Celluloid—A thermoplastic, made from cellulose and camphor, possibly invented as a substitute for ivory and widely used at one time as the base material for photographic film. Originally a trademark of the Celluloid Manufacturing Company, registered in 1870.

Dry ice—Frozen carbon dioxide, so called because it does not melt, returning instead to a gaseous form as it warms. Originally trademarked by the Dry Ice Corporation of America in 1925.

Escalator—The moving staircase that makes shopping malls possible, invented in 1897 by Charles Seeberger and first used as an amusement ride at Coney Island. Escalator, combining the Greek *scala*, "steps," with the ending of *elevator*, remained a trademark of the Otis Elevator Company until 1950, when it became a generic term.

Heroin—A painkiller of the opiate family, synthesized from morphine and technically known as *diacetylmorphine*, heroin was invented in London in 1874 and trademarked by Bayer AG as Heroin (from the German, meaning "heroic treatment") in 1910. Ironically, heroin was first marketed as a nonaddictive pain reliever and used in children's cough medicine.

LP—Meaning "long-playing phonograph record," LP was originally trademarked by Columbia Records but fairly quickly slipped into generic use.

Mimeograph—Precursor of photocopying machines, the Mimeograph (from the Greek *mimeesthai*, "to imitate," plus *graph*, "writing") was once a trademarked name but widely used as a generic term for a variety of duplication methods.

Webster's Dictionary—The first truly American dictionary was *An American Dictionary of the English Language*, published by Noah Webster in 1828. After Webster's death, George and Charles Merriam bought the rights to the dictionary and to use Webster's name, but "Webster's" eventually became so synonymous with "dictionary" in popular usage that the name lost its trademark status. Today any dictionary may call itself "Webster's," but those published by Merriam-Webster are considered the most direct descendants of Noah Webster's dictionary.

Zipper—Invented (in its modern form) in 1917 as the "Separable Fastener" by Gideon Sundback, an employee of the Universal Fastener Company. The trademark Zipper was coined in 1923 by the B. F. Goodrich Company, but eventually *zipper* became a victim of its own linguistic genius and was ruled a generic term.

Among the living, so far: The following brand names are often used as generic terms but remain, for the moment at least, protected trademarks. When in doubt, watch your step—even ZIP Code is a registered trademark of the United States Postal Service.

Aqua-Lung	Pablum
AstroTurf	Plexiglas
Baggies	Popsicle
Band-Aid	Post-it
Crock-Pot	Quonset
Dixie cups	Realtor
Dumpster	Rolodex
Formica	Spackle
GoKart	Styrofoam
Google	Tabasco
Jacuzzi	Taser
Laundromat	Teflon
Magic Marker	TelePrompTer
Muzak	VHS
Ouija board	Walkman

Lysol

If anyone doubts the difference a dapper product name can make, consider the case of Lysol, the classic disinfectant.

Louis Lehn and Frederick Fink had founded the pharmaceutical firm of Lehn & Fink in New York City in 1874, and had built a solid business largely through importing drugs and sundries (including high-powered European lavender) to the United States.

At the turn of the century, Lehn & Fink stumbled onto a new disinfectant becoming popular in Europe and began importing it. But the name the concoction came with—Liquor Cresolis Compositus—was unwieldy and clearly unmarketable.

At this point Albert Plaut, who had acquired the company in 1898, faced his first serious test and came up with a winner. Plaut renamed the solution Lysol, a combination of its two main ingredients, lye and cresol. Platoons of Lehn & Fink salesmen fanned out across the land bearing Lysol, and thousands of samples were mailed to doctors in one of the first such mass advertising campaigns. Within a few years Lysol had become, and remains, the most popular brand-name disinfectant.

Microsoft

For a company that makes the software that runs most of the world's computers (and has been accused of trying to run the world), Microsoft seems to have had some surprising difficulty deciding how to spell its own name.

When founders Bill Gates and Paul Allen were just starting out in 1975, Gates wrote a letter to Allen referring to their nascent partnership by the name Micro-Soft, an abbreviation of "microcomputer software." At that time, the dawn of the age of personal computing, any computer smaller than a bathtub was considered to be "micro," from the Latin for "small." Slightly larger computers were dubbed minicomputers, a melding of "miniature computer."

Versions of the name bounced back and forth in company literature like typographical tennis balls over the next year or so, ranging from the hyphenated forms "Micro-Soft" and "Micro-soft" to the now-fashionable irregularly capitalized "MicroSoft" to the no-frills "Microsoft." But when it came time to incorporate their creation in 1976, Gates and Allen went with the simplest form, Microsoft, which a cynic might say was the last uncomplicated thing their company ever did.

Motorola

Most people would consider parking a car at the curb and cranking up the radio rude or worse. But when Paul Galvin did it in 1930, it was brilliant guerrilla marketing.

When Galvin founded his Galvin Manufacturing Corporation in 1928, the timing could not have been worse. The Chicago company had early success with its "battery eliminator," which allowed radio owners to run their sets on household current, but the stock market crash of 1929 threw the continued existence of Galvin's enterprise into serious doubt.

Searching for a new product to revitalize his company, Galvin learned that some auto shops were doing makeshift installations of radios in customers' cars. Galvin realized that a radio made specifically for cars, easy to install and insulated from interference, could be a winner. He rushed his staff to work on the project, and they produced a working model just in time for the 1930 Radio Manufacturers Association convention in Atlantic City, New Jersey.

Unfortunately, Galvin lacked the funds to rent a booth at the convention, so he had his engineers rig an external speaker to the radio mounted in his own Studebaker, drove to the convention, parked out front, and cranked up the volume. A crowd quickly gathered, and as Galvin pitched his product, his wife took down the names of distributors interested in selling the radios.

One hurdle now remained—what to call the gizmo? Gavin polled his team of designers, and they quickly settled on Motorola, combining a sense of motion from "moto" with sound from the suffix -ola, well known in the trade names of Victrola phonographs and Pianola player pianos.

The combination of sound and motion has turned out to be a corporate mantra for Motorola, Inc. Today a leader in mobile communications technology, from police radios to wireless Internet networks, the company is probably best known to consumers for its cell phones. In fact, a Motorola scientist, Dr. Martin Cooper, is credited with developing the first truly portable wireless telephone in 1975.

Muzak

Your call is important to us. One of our award-winning service representatives will be with you as soon as possible. Please do not hang up and call back, because if you do you're likely to miss this lovely rendition of the Clash's classic "Rock the Casbah" by the talented Kenny G.

From all indications, General George Owen Squier (1865–1934) was a thoroughly nice guy, so he's probably not roasting in hell to the mellifluous tunes of the Muzak he invented. But a lot of people seem to wish he were.

Squier, a two-star general and electrical engineer, patented a method of distributing music over electrical lines in 1920 and called his invention Muzak, combining *music* with the name of a company he admired greatly—Kodak. Muzak's first big success was due to the emerging skyscraper craze. Builders discovered that nervous passengers on the new-fangled elevators were soothed by Squier's music, and soon music was being piped into offices and factories as well. By the 1950s, Squier's invention was becoming omnipresent in stores, as merchants discovered that constant background music encouraged buying. Today 80 million people hear Muzak all over the world on a given day, and there are hundreds of different Muzak streams, now delivered via satellite, ranging from pop to classical music.

Not everyone, to put it mildly, has been a Muzak fan. Although Muzak is a trademarked brand name, like Q-tips and

Kleenex, it has also become a widely used generic term. Perhaps unfairly, the lowercase form "muzak" has become synonymous with bland, vaguely annoying music, especially when used as background music in stores and restaurants (or to torment customers placed on indefinite hold). In trendier precincts, Muzak and its synonyms have become the critical kiss of death, as when REM's Michael Stipe referred to the Beatles' music as elevator music a few years ago.

Nikon

"I've got a Nikon camera, I love to take photographs," sang Paul Simon in his 1973 hit song "Kodachrome," thereby boosting sales of both Kodak's flagship color slide film and a camera brand that very few Americans had heard of until just a few years earlier.

But Nikon had been well known in the optical industry since its formation as a consortium of three leading Japanese optical manufacturers as Nippon Kogaku K.K. in 1917. For the first several decades of its existence, Nippon Kogaku concentrated on manufacturing high-quality microscopes, telescopes, binoculars, and surveying instruments. In the 1930s, following the growing popularity of 35mm cameras pioneered by Leitz in its Leica cameras, Nippon Kogaku began producing small cameras and lenses under the Nikon name, derived from a melding of the name Nippon Kogaku. American photojournalists were introduced to Nikon cameras while covering the Korean War in the early 1950s, and when Nikon introduced the legendary Nikon F single-lens reflex camera system in 1959, the brand quickly attained the respect among professional photographers formerly reserved for Leica. Nikon today is known for its high-quality cameras as well as a wide array of scientific and technical optical devices.

Pentium

In 1993, Intel needed a name for its new-generation microprocessor, the successor to its flagship 486 chip. Past corporate practice would have made the choice a no-brainer—just call it the 586, following the model of Intel's previous 286, 386, and 486.

But Intel had discovered the down side to such no-frills naming. Annoyed at competitor AMD's practice of marketing its versions of Intel's chips by simply tacking "AMD" onto Intel's number (AMD486, etc.), Intel had sued AMD for trademark infringement. Intel argued that if Boeing could trademark airplane model numbers such as 707, 727, etc., it should own "486" and its ilk.

But AMD pointed out that Intel had never actually called its chip the 486. It had marketed the chips under its parts' numbers: in the case of the 486, as the I80486. Intel might own the whole number I80486, AMD argued, but not just the last three digits 486. Intel lost the case and learned an expensive lesson: no more number names.

Intel turned to Lexicon Branding, Inc., the Sausalito, California, company that has also created the names PowerBook and DeskJet, to come up with a trademark that could be protected. At the end of a three-month process of combing through thousands of possibilities, Intel and Lexicon finally had their name: Pentium, derived from the Greek *penta*, meaning "five" (reflecting the 586 series designation). According to Lexicon founder and president David Placek, the strength of Pentium may lie in its nonspecific, nontechnical sound. In an interview with *Computerworld* magazine in 1998, Placek explained, "The biggest mistake companies make today is being too descriptive with their names. If you look at the name Pentium, the difference between that and an alternative name, such as Prochip, is that Prochip is very descriptive and one-dimensional. . . . With a name like Pentium, you can talk about speed and power and innovation. It lets you build a personality for the product over time."

After initially being taken a bit aback by the unconventional name, the computer industry (and, more important, consumers) took a shine to Pentium, but as progress marched on, another problem arose. To follow the Latinate *pent-* form, the new sixth generation of processor should rightly have been called the Sexium, which Intel felt might be a bit much. So the Pentium, a name that had been so successful that Intel didn't want to give it up anyway, begat the Pentium II, Pentium III, and so on.

Polaroid

Dr. Edwin Land's daughter had a good question. It was 1944, and Land, the leading developer of the synthetic polarized material still used today in sunglasses and hundreds of other products, was on vacation with his family in New Mexico. His daughter, however, wanted to know why she couldn't see the pictures they were taking right away, rather than having to send the film to a photofinisher to be developed. Land tackled the problem over the next three years, and in 1948 announced the debut of the Polaroid Land camera, which used self-developing film that produced finished picture in sixty seconds.

The name Polaroid, combining the "pola" from *polarized* with the then popular suffix *-oid* (meaning "utilizing or characteristic of"), had been coined in 1935 to market Land's polarized sunglass lenses and, in 1937, was adopted as a corporate name. But while the Polaroid Corporation developed thousands of other products over the following decades, to the American public Polaroid almost immediately came to mean "instant picture." Polaroid still produces instant film cameras and a wide range of other products.

Pyrex

Sometimes trade names don't play by the rules, and the official explanation of Pyrex, Corning Incorporated's trade name for the heatproof glass invented by Corning scientists Eugene Sullivan and William Taylor and patented by the company in 1915, is not the one that would please an etymologist. If it had been dreamed up by a linguist, Pyrex would be a combination of the Greek *pyr,* meaning "fire," and the Latin *rex,* or "king," giving us "fire king," a logical name for glass cookware that won't shatter in the heat of an oven. Pyrex is such a nice name that most linguistic authorities would probably have waived the rule against combining Latin and Greek roots.

Corning itself, however, says that the name Pyrex was first used for an early heatproof pie plate that had originally been dubbed the "Py-right." But Corning at that point was fond of ending its product names in *-ex* (e.g., Nonex), and so the name was changed to Pyrex.

In any case, the secret of Pyrex turns out to lie in adding boron to the glass mixture, lowering its thermal coefficient and making it more resistant to heat. Because Pyrex also contracts and expands less than regular glass, it was used in 1934 to make the famous 200-inch mirror of the Mount Palomar telescope in California.

Random House

Only in the publishing industry (or possibly casino management) could an enterprise not only survive but flourish with the word *random* in its name. *Random,* meaning "lacking a definite plan, purpose, or pattern," is not a word stockholders like to see in an annual report, let alone on the front door of their investment. And in today's high-stakes book market, when the successors to the venerable firm of Harper & Row are in such a hurry they haven't even time to put a space in HarperCollins, it's unlikely that Bertelsmann AG, the conglomerate that has owned Random House since 1998, would ever be crazy enough to come up with Random as a name.

But it was a different world back in 1925 when Bennett Cerf and Donald Klopfer, both then in their twenties, purchased The Modern Library, a line of classic American literary works, from its publisher, Horace Liveright. Cerf and Klopfer were more interested in great literature than market share, and within two years had decided to expand their enterprise to publish a few original works as well as the classics. Since they were determined to publish whatever they found worthy without adhering to a strict timetable or sales quota, they announced that they would be publishing "at random," and puckishly called their new publishing house "Random House." The logo for Random House was designed by a friend, the great American artist Rockwell Kent, who later illustrated the firm's editions of *Moby-Dick* and *Candide,* among other classic works.

For a publisher whose very name seems synonymous with "laid back," Random House quickly found itself in the spotlight in 1934 by publishing James Joyce's then banned masterpiece *Ulysses,* a move that led to a highly publicized court fight with government censors.

Rolex

One of the world's premier watch brands, Rolex scored its first public relations coup because of a disputed swim across the English Channel.

In 1905, Bavarian-born Hans Wilsdorf and his brother-in-law started a watchmaking firm in London under the name Wilsdorf & Davis, importing Swiss watch movements and parts and assembling them into completed timepieces. Since there were many such firms at the time, Wilsdorf & Davis decided to specialize in wristwatches, then just gaining acceptance in a market dominated by pocket watches.

Wilsdorf was dedicated to improving watch technology, and he experimented with a variety of new designs, marketing them under such names as the Unicorn, the Marconi, the Rolco, and the Tudor. In 1908, he was searching for a name for a new model and came up with Rolex, which he immediately recognized had all the makings of a great name: it was short, easy to pronounce, suggested forward motion, and, to Wilsdorf at least, was reminiscent of the sound made by winding a watch.

When the outbreak of World War I a few years later made anything German-sounding unpopular (including sauerkraut, which was renamed "victory cabbage" for the duration of the war), Wilsdorf & Davis decided to change the name of their company to Rolex.

In 1926, after many years of research and development, Wilsdorf produced the world's first waterproof watch, the

Rolex Oyster. In 1927, Mercedes Gleitze became the first English woman to swim the English Channel, but her feat was widely disputed, so she offered to repeat her swim to appease the skeptics. Wilsdorf recognized a golden opportunity, and asked her to wear his new Oyster on her second swim. When Mercedes Gleitze emerged from the Channel with both her record and the Rolex intact, Wilsdorf splashed a full-page ad across the front of London's *Daily Mail*, and the Rolex legendary reputation for quality was born.

Scotch Tape

Scotch brand tape, notwithstanding the tartan design featured on its packaging, has no connection to Scotland. In fact, the first use of "Scotch" to refer to tape manufactured by 3M was intended as an insult to the product.

The first Scotch tape was not, oddly enough, the transparent tape we usually think of today when we hear "Scotch tape." In 1925, a young engineer named Richard Drew working for the Minnesota Mining and Manufacturing Company (now 3M) invented the first masking tape to help auto body painters keep a straight edge between colors when painting two-tone cars. It was a great idea and instantly popular with painters, but unfortunately, when 3M first began to manufacture the tape, it decided to put adhesive only on the edges of the tape, not the whole surface. This made the tape easier to remove but also gave it a distressing tendency to fall off before the painting job was done. According to 3M lore, one painter testing the tape became so frustrated with its unpredictable performance that he angrily thrust the tape back into Drew's hands, saying "Take this tape back to those Scotch bosses of yours and tell them to put more adhesive on it!"

The use of "Scotch" as a slang adjective meaning "stingy" had a history at that time dating back to England in the seventeenth century, and was one of a number of national slurs, including many targeting the Dutch and the French, rooted in the national rivalries of the period. Reflecting England's ambiguous attitude toward its northern neighbor, almost anything deemed nasty, stingy, or penny-pinching was dubbed "Scotch" in England, from Scotch blessing (a severe scolding) to Scotch marriage (a common-law marriage) to Scotch coffee (hot water flavored by a burned biscuit). While many such "Scotch" terms had faded away over the centuries, "Scotch" as a general slang synonym for "stingy" was still alive and well in the United States in the 1920s.

Rather than taking offense at the labeling of its masking tape as "Scotch," 3M embraced the name and applied it to its entire line of tapes, and when five years later Richard Drew invented the first transparent cellulose tape, it was known from Day One as Scotch Transparent Tape.

Scrabble

The real mystery about the invention of Scrabble is why Frank Capra didn't turn it into a movie.

Fade-in on a Queens, New York, walk-up apartment in the

depths of the 1930s Depression. Alfred Mosher Butts, architect, has lost his job at a time when new jobs are impossible to find. Desperate to make ends meet, Alfred Butts decides to invent a game. A methodical man, Butts does his homework first and spends hours analyzing existing games. He finds that they fall into three main categories: move games (chess, checkers, etc.), number games (dice, bingo), and word games like anagrams. Butts decides his best bet is to combine an element of chance, as in dice, with an exercise of skill and knowledge, as in word games.

For the next few months, Alfred Butts studies *The New York Times,* the *New York Herald Tribune,* and *The Saturday Evening Post,* keeping painstaking statistics on the frequency with which each letter in the alphabet appears. Armed with his analysis, Butts creates a game he calls Lexico, a hybrid of anagrams and a crossword puzzle, using small plywood letter tiles and little racks made of baseboard molding. He sells Lexico himself for $1.50 and approaches all the major game companies, hoping to find a distributor to boost Lexico into the national market. They all turn him down.

But Alfred Butts perseveres, adds a playing board to his game, and renames it Criss-Cross Words. Unfortunately, he has created another flop, or so it seems. By now it is 1947 and Butts meets a man named James Brunot, who buys the rights to his game in exchange for royalties on units sold. Brunot fiddles with the game a bit and decides to rename it Scrabble, a word meaning "to scramble, grope at hurriedly, to write quickly, or scribble," derived from the Dutch *schrabbelen,* meaning "to scratch."

And now it's Brunot's turn to face a flop. Scrabble is limping along, selling 2,400 sets in 1949 and losing money. Until, that is, the president of Macy's plays the game while on vacation and orders all his stores to carry it. Bang, zoom. Orders up the wazoo, coming in faster than Brunot could make the games. By 1954, Selchow and Righter, a well-known game manufacturer to whom Brunot licensed Scrabble in 1952, was selling more than 3.8 million sets a year. America goes Scrabble crazy, and never really stops. Today there's a Scrabble set in one out of every three U.S. homes, and Scrabble, now owned by Hasbro Inc., is an American icon. And Alfred Butts, no longer "scrabbling" to make a living, lives to age ninety-three, playing his beloved Scrabble right up to the end.

Slinky

> What walks down stairs, alone or in pairs, and makes a
>   slinkity sound?
> A spring, a spring, a marvelous thing—everyone knows it's
>   Slinky.
> It's Slinky, it's Slinky, for fun it's a wonderful toy.
> It's fun for a girl and a boy.
> It's fun for a girl and a boy.

Maybe it was that "slinkity" sound that drove poor Richard James around the bend.

James, a naval engineer working with tension springs, dropped one of them one day in 1943 and noticed that the spring kept moving, pulling itself end-over-end across the floor. James mentioned to his wife, Betty, that the spring might make a good children's toy, and together they spent the next two years perfecting the gizmo.

Betty was the one who came up with the Slinky name after searching a dictionary and settling on the word meaning "stealthy, sinuous, and graceful of movement."

Richard and Betty first demonstrated the Slinky at Gimbel's department store in Philadelphia at Christmas, 1945, and were so apprehensive that Betty arranged for a friend to show up and get things rolling by buying the first one. That proved to be unnecessary, as within ninety minutes their entire stock of four hundred Slinkys had been sold and Slinky was off and hopping as America's newest toy craze.

In 1960, however, Richard abandoned his wife, six children, and the Slinky empire to join a religious cult in Bolivia. Betty took over the company, repaired its finances (which had suffered from Richard's contributions to the cult), and began to advertise Slinky on TV with the snappy Slinky jingle. Slinky sales took off again and have never stopped. Close to 300 million Slinkys have been sold in the years since and it's still a bargain—originally sold for a dollar in 1945, Slinkys go for just $2.99 today.

Sony

Most companies post some sort of corporate history on their Web site, ranging from a brief paragraph to a page or two explaining how their founder's childhood dreams and youthful struggles culminated in America's favorite laundry soap or dessert pudding. Sony Corporation, with the same attention to detail that has brought it world dominance in the electronics industry (but probably driven company copy editors to drink), devotes more than 150 Web pages in thirty-seven separate chapters to an exhaustive blow-by-blow narrative of the company's history.

The story of how Sony became Sony really isn't that complicated, although it was not a name that was instantly popular even within the company itself. For the first twelve years of its existence after its founding in 1946, the company was known as Tokyo Tsushin Kogyo (Totsuko for short), meaning Tokyo Telecommunications Engineering Corporation. Founders Masar Ibuka and Akio Morita started out in business making electric rice cookers and heated cushions just after World War II but had progressed by the mid-1950s to producing tape recorders and the first transistor radios, and realized that their company's future lay in the global marketplace. Morita in particular felt that a new name was needed, something a global consumer would find easier to pronounce and spell.

Morita's choice was Sony, a combination of the Latin root *son,* meaning "sound," and the English word *sonny,* which in Morita's opinion carried connotations of youth, energy, and affection. The company had used the name Soni on its recording tape for several years, but Morita feared that Soni would be pronounced "so-nigh," and the alternative spelling Sonny might come out as "son-ny," perilously close to the Japanese word *son,* meaning "loss." But Sony seemed impossible to mis-pronounce and was short enough to be unforgettable.

For a Japanese company to pick a new, non-Japanese name at that time, however, was unprecedented and considered very ill-advised. Totsuko's own principal banker was bluntly in-credulous: "It's taken you ten years since the company's foun-dation to make the name Tokyo Tsushin Kogyo widely known in the trade. After all this time, what is your intention by pro-posing such a nonsensical change?"

Morita, however, was adamant, and refused to modify the new name to "Sony Electronics Corporation" or the like, feel-ing that the company should not limit its future endeavors (cars? airplanes?) with unnecessary qualifiers. Morita, of course, was right, and within a few years two things had hap-pened: Totsuko was forgotten, and Sony was on its way to be-coming a household word around the world.

Swatch

On the surface, the name Swatch for the innovative line of un-orthodox, brightly colored plastic Swiss-made watches that first hit the market in 1983 couldn't be simpler. The name is just short for "Swiss watch." But perhaps Swatch really should be known as The Watch That Saved the Swiss Watch Industry But Almost Went to Market with a Really Awful Name.

By the late 1970s, Swiss watchmakers were in a pickle and sinking fast. Competition from Japanese makers had cut the Swiss worldwide market share for watches from 43 to 15 percent in just a decade, and although the Swiss had invented the new quartz movement, it was Japanese watchmakers who had used it to conquer the global watch market. Swiss watch firms were almost ready to throw in the towel and sell their venerable brand names to the highest bidder.

In 1978, adding technological insult to the economic injury, a Japanese firm introduced the thinnest watch ever made, just 2.5mm thick. Faced with a challenge and a hefty dose of last-ditch determination, designers at the firm of ETA SA invented an entirely new way to construct a watch in a one-piece case. Within just five months they revealed the new Kaliber 999, the world's thinnest gold wristwatch at only .98mm thick.

Apart from giving a boost to Swiss pride, the new one-piece manufacturing method piqued the interest of ETA engineers, who used the new design to manufacture the world's first low-cost plastic watch in 1981. The preproduction code name for the gold Kaliber 999 had been "Delirium tremens," playfully likening the awesome challenge of beating the Japanese to the hallucinating "shakes" suffered by alcoholics. So the ETA engineers dubbed the new plastic watch the Delirium Vulgaris (or "People's Delirium"), and the watch actually debuted to the public as the Vulgaris. Fortunately, more sober heads prevailed, and, renamed Swatch, the little plastic watch that could conquered the world and restored Swiss watchmaking, today controlling 53 percent of the world market, to prominence.

TAG Heuer

The "Heuer" in TAG Heuer rhymes with *lawyer*, surely a cosmic coincidence since TAG Heuer watches have attained a status among the affluent equaled only by Rolex.

For most of its history, the company was known as simply Heuer, after Swiss founder Edouard Heuer. A traditional watchmaker at the outset, Heuer soon developed an interest in precision timing for sporting events, and in 1916 he invented the first stopwatch capable of timing down to 1/100th of a second. The company he founded has since been the official timekeeper at several Olympic Games, many Formula One auto races, and the Indianapolis 500.

The "TAG" in the company's name is a reflection of a convoluted change in ownership in the 1980s. In 1983, Edouard Heuer's heirs decided to sell the company to the French firm Piaget, itself a maker of upscale watches and jewelry. But within two years, Piaget sold a controlling interest in Heuer to a Saudi Arabian investment group known as Techniques d'Avant Garde, or TAG for short.

Teflon

It wasn't anything you or I couldn't have accomplished with our childhood chemistry sets, given corporate backing and a thousand years or so.

On April 6, 1938, Dr. Roy J. Plunkett was fiddling around

with some variants of Freon gas at the New Jersey laboratories of DuPont. "Hey, I think I'll check on that sample of frozen, compressed tetrafluoroethylene I saw in the back of the fridge last week," thought Dr. Plunkett, and so he did. To his astonishment, he discovered that his frozen chunk of tetrafluoroethylene had spontaneously polymerized into nothing less than polytetrafluoroethylene (from the Latin meaning "many tetrafluoroethylenes").

This metamorphosis was not only unexpected but fortuitous as well, for polytetrafluoroethylene turned out to be The Most Slippery Material in Existence. And as soon as he managed to get a firm grip on his sample of polytetrafluoroethylene, Dr. Plunkett celebrated his discovery by abbreviating its name to PTFE.

Unfortunately, from a marketing standpoint, PTFE sounded far too much like someone spitting out watermelon seeds, so the naming gnomes at DuPont decided to call the material Teflon, coupling the *t*, and *f* from tetrafluoroethylene with the "lon" of *nylon*, also a DuPont invention.

Teflon today is used in thousands of nonstick products and industrial applications, and in 1990 President George H. W. Bush awarded DuPont a special medal for the company's pioneering work in polymers, including the invention of Teflon. Ironically, just a few years earlier a genericized "teflon" had entered the political vocabulary as a derogatory adjective applied to politicians to whom scandal did not stick.

Tupperware

For Earl Tupper, coming up with a better idea for food storage was the easy part. To sell his creation to consumers, Tupper had to first adopt a whole new approach to marketing.

A former DuPont engineer, Tupper knew his plastics, having spent World War II manufacturing plastic gas mask components for the U.S. government. After the war, Tupper began experimenting with molded polyethylene, a strong, lightweight, flexible plastic with none of the usual "plastic" odor. Realizing that home refrigerators, which were just then coming on the market, had a tendency to dry out food stored in them, Tupper designed bowls of polyethylene in pastel colors for food storage, and after much experimentation even arrived at a clever way to create an airtight seal between the bowl and its lid. By building slack into the lid allowing it to be "burped" when it was sealed, the bowl created a slight vacuum and kept food remarkably fresh.

The bowls worked well, and Tupper found that department and hardware stores were eager to sell his new Tupperware bowls. The only problem was that postwar consumers, having learned to regard anything made of plastic as "cheap," balked at Tupper's prices. And even those who tried Tupper's bowls often couldn't figure out how to make the special sealing feature work. Sales slumped as the bowls gathered dust on store shelves. America didn't seem ready for a pricey plastic food bowl with a steep learning curve.

Enter Bonnie Wise, a Chicago woman who had been selling Stanley Home Products directly to her neighbors at "demonstration parties" held in her customers' own living rooms. After receiving a set of the bowls as a gift, Wise figured out (after three days) how they worked and realized that all that was missing from Tupper's brilliant invention was a real person to explain how it worked. Wise was ready to be that person, and added Tupper's bowls to her sales kit. Seeing her immediate success with "Tupperware parties," Tupper promptly hired Wise, who recruited more home sellers, and under the new "party plan," sales zoomed. Today a Tupperware party starts somewhere in the world every two seconds.

Velcro

Next time the *rrrriippp* sound of a Velcro fastener gets on your nerves, take it up with your dog.

Back in the early 1940s, Swiss inventor George de Mestral decided to take his loyal dog for a walk. Mestral's dog, as dogs are wont to do, led his master through some brambles and brush. Upon returning home, Mestral discovered that both his trousers and the dog were covered with prickly burrs.

A lesser man might simply have thrown his trousers in the corner and shaved the dog, but Mestral was a Swiss inventor, and took his responsibility to science seriously. Studying the burrs under his microscope, Mestral discovered that the secret of a burr's dogged stickiness lay in the tiny hook at the tip of each of its little spines that grabbed and held tight to the loops of thread in Mestral's trousers.

Mimicking nature, Mestral then designed a reusable fastening system with two sides: one with tiny hooks like the burr, the other with plenty of fabric loops like his trousers. The resulting product was dubbed Velcro, combining the French *velours,* "velvet" (referring to the smooth looped side) with *crochet,* "hook."

Manufacturing Velcro turned out to be a tricky business, and it took quite a while to get the technology of making those tiny hooks just right, but today Velcro, manufactured by Velcro Industries B.V., is used in thousands of products, including, of course, dog coats.

WD-40

Don't ask what this stuff does. It apparently does everything, more than one million cans of it are sold every week, and four out of five households in the United States have a can kicking around somewhere.

WD-40 was invented in 1953 by scientists at the Rocket Chemical Company in San Diego. The company name might sound like typical business hype, but these folks were seriously searching for a way to prevent corrosion to missile parts, and in WD-40 they hit the jackpot. By 1959 their invention was being used by the U.S. government to prevent corrosion in Atlas missiles.

But that was just the beginning of WD-40's career. Workers at the WD-40 plant began smuggling the stuff out and using it at home, discovering in the process that WD-40 would protect their tools from rust, lubricate and rustproof darn near anything, and even loosen nuts and bolts rusted tight. The makers of WD-40 now boast a list of more than two thousand uses for the product, including one case when police officers used WD-40 to free a naked burglar trapped in an air-conditioning vent.

For a miracle product, the origin of WD-40's name is surprisingly humble. The scientists who developed it were looking for a "water displacement" substance to drive away moisture and prevent rust, and it took them forty tries to get it right, so WD-40 simply stands for "Water Displacement—40th Attempt."

WD-40 is still produced by the gang at Rocket Chemical, renamed WD-40 Company, Inc. in 1973, which also manufactures 3-IN-ONE oil and several other products.

Xerox

If you've ever spent an entire Monday morning trying to get your office photocopying machine to stop spitting out Rorschach tests instead of that memo to your boss, you'll be able to identify with Chester Carlson, the man who invented the Xerox technology in 1938. It took him more than twenty years to get anyone to pay attention to an invention that truly revolutionized office life.

Chester Carlson was just getting by as a young patent attorney in Depression-era New York City when he decided to supplement his income with a little inventing on the side.

From his experience working in a large office, Carlson knew that making copies of documents was an expensive, time-consuming chore, and realized that anyone who came up with a solution simpler than the messy photocopying process then in use would have a winner.

What Carlson didn't realize was that even after he had spent years establishing the principles and basic method of making "dry" copies, it would be nearly impossible to interest any company in further developing his "electrophotographic" invention. Finally, in 1944, he convinced the Battelle Memorial Institute in Columbus, Ohio, to sign a development contract. Battelle soon turned to a small photographic manufacturer, the Haloid Company of Rochester, New York, for help, and together they turned Carlson's invention into the first practical office copier.

It had taken ten long years of struggle for Carlson's process to hit the market, but now, on the doorstep of success, both Haloid and Battelle realized that "Electrophotographic Copy Machine" was not exactly a catchy product name. So they tracked down a classics professor at the nearby Ohio State University, who after some thought suggested "xerography," from the Greek words for "dry writing" (as opposed to the "wet" chemical methods it would hopefully be replacing). In 1949, Haloid introduced the Xerox Copier (oddly capitalized for the first model as XeroX) and, after the enormous success of the machine and subsequent models, changed its corporate name first to Haloid Xerox and finally, in 1961, to simply Xerox Corporation.

Yahoo!

There are two overlapping explanations of why David Filo and Jerry Yang, the founders of the Yahoo! Web portal and search engine, picked that particular name back in 1994. The first explains Yahoo! as an acronym for Yet Another Hierarchical Officious Oracle, a jocular reference to the original Internet Oracle, a humorous collective question-answering enterprise dating back to the early days of the Internet. As Yahoo! (the exclamation point is part of the trademark) helps millions of Internet users find what they're looking for, it could be considered a similar sort of oracle.

But the official corporate history posted at the Yahoo! Web page maintains that the name Yahoo! was also chosen because the site's two founders liked the dictionary definition of *yahoo* ("rude, unsophisticated, uncouth"), and Filo and Yang have been quoted as saying that they consider themselves yahoos. If so, they may be the world's richest yahoos, a fact that must take a bit of the sting out of what has always been a very pejorative term.

Yo-Yo

The Yo-Yo boasts the distinction of being considered the second-oldest toy in the world (after dolls), having been invented in Greece at least 2,500 years ago. So the little toy that rides up and down a string would seem an unlikely candidate for a trademark dispute over its name. But the humble Yo-Yo was once the subject of a hotly contested court fight over who owned the Yo-Yo name.

The toy now known as the Yo-Yo first appeared in Europe around 1800 and was known by a number of names; in England it was called the bandalore or quiz, and in France it was known as the *incroyable* or *l'emigrette*.

The Yo-Yo had also been popular in the Philippines for hundreds of years, and it was a Filipino immigrant who actually started the Yo-Yo craze that swept the United States starting in the 1930s. Pedro Flores remembered the toy from his homeland and began making and selling them in the 1920s. Flores's toy caught the eye of Donald Duncan, an inventor (Eskimo Pies), entrepreneur (the first practical parking meter), and marketing whiz. Duncan bought the rights to Flores's product and trademarked the name Yo-Yo. He then set out to drive America Yo-Yo crazy, and succeeded. Within a few years, Duncan's factory was churning out 3,600 Yo-Yos per hour and selling three million in a single month in Philadelphia.

The peak year for Yo-Yo sales was 1962, with Duncan's sales topping $7 million. Unfortunately, by now the company had competition, and Duncan was forced to defend its trademarked Yo-Yo name in a court battle with Royal Tops.

Duncan lost the case. The court ruled that Yo-Yo was a generic term, a well-known term in the Tagalog language of the Philippines (meaning "come back"), and could not be trademarked.

But worse news was to come, as the Yo-Yo fad faded and the

legal expenses of the court case drove both Duncan and Royal Tops into bankruptcy.

The Yo-Yo almost disappeared from the American scene for the next twenty-four years. But the early 1990s saw a rebirth and renewed popularity for the Yo-Yo, as Duncan, now under new ownership, was there to lead the development of America's favorite toy into a serious sport with annual international competitions.

CARS

Hummer

It's a bird, it's a plane, it's an all-terrain vehicle that will bring out your inner Lewis and Clark and take you to the top of life's mountains. Or it's a gas-guzzling behemoth too wide for the road and a menace to anyone driving a normal car. Most vehicles are largely a matter of personal taste or utilitarian choice, but the Hummer is an in-your-face social statement that inspires either longing looks of envy or muttered curses of annoyance.

Much of the Hummer's appeal, to those who find it appealing, comes from its military lineage, as does its name. The original H1 Hummer was simply a civilian version of the U.S. military's High Mobility Multi-Purpose Wheeled Vehicle, made famous during the first Gulf War in 1991 and better known in the military as the Humvee. The more recent H2 Hummer, produced by General Motors (who bought the original Humvee manufacturer), is a tamed-down, more consumer-oriented version (gas engine instead of diesel, Bose stereo, etc.) of the H1.

Motoring Monikers

Names of American automobile brands are remarkable if for no other reason than that so few drivers have any idea of who Louis Chevrolet or Antoine de la Mothe Cadillac might have been. The Japanese makers are a bit more adventurous, occasionally naming their cars after Zoroastrian gods or star clusters. Here are a few of the stories behind the major automobile brands.

Audi—When August Horch, founder of the brand in 1909, lost the right to use his own name in the car business, he translated *horch*, which means "listen" in German, into Latin, which gave the world Audi cars.

BMW—Stands for Bayerische Motoren Werke, or Bavarian Motor Works.

Bentley—Named for Walter Owen Bentley, automotive engineer and founder of Bentley Motors.

Buick—Named for David Dunbar Buick, Scottish immigrant who founded the Buick Motor Company. Despite creating one of the most successful auto brands, Dunbar died penniless.

Chrysler—Named for Walter Chrysler, onetime head of the Buick Motor Company who oversaw its integration into General Motors.

Cadillac—Named for Antoine de la Mothe Cadillac (1658–1730), French explorer and founder of Detroit.

Chevrolet—Named for Louis Chevrolet, a French racing driver whose automotive designs impressed William Durant, then head of Buick.

Dodge—Named for John and Horace Dodge, bicycle-making brothers who eventually worked up to making their own cars.

Ferrari—Named for Enzo Ferrari, Italian racing driver who became a legendary designer of sports and racing cars.

Fiat—An acronym for Fabrica Italiana Automobili Torini, meaning "Italian Car Factory of Turin." In Italian, perhaps not coincidentally, *in un fiat* means "in an instant." Among the car's detractors, however, Fiat is said to stand for "Fix it again, Tony."

Ford—Named for Henry Ford, founder of the Ford Motor Company and inventor of modern mass-production techniques. Chevy partisans maintain that Ford actually stands for Fix or Repair Daily.

Honda—Named for Soichiro Honda, who began making motorcycles in postwar Japan and eventually revolutionized the compact car industry.

Lincoln—Named for Abraham Lincoln, oddly enough the only U.S. president ever so honored.

Mazda—Named after Ahura Mazda, the highest Zoroastrian god, by company founder Jujiro Matsuda, to whose name it also bears a resemblance. Zoroastrianism, founded in Persia about 1000 B.C., is one of the world's oldest monotheistic religions.

Mercury—Named for the Roman god Mercury, messenger of the gods and associated with speed.

Mitsubishi—Founded as a Japanese shipping firm in 1870, Mitsubishi is Japanese for "three diamonds," the company's symbol.

Nissan—Short form of the company's original name, Nichon Sangio (meaning "Japanese Industry"). Nissan cars were, until the 1980s, marketed under the name Datsun, "Dat" being an acronym made from the initials of the three founders' last names.

Oldsmobile—Named for Ransom E. Olds, pioneer automobile engineer and inventor who established the first car company in Detroit, the Olds Motor Company, in 1897.

Rolls-Royce—Named for Charles Stewart Rolls and Frederick Henry Royce, who founded the company in 1906. Rolls, also a pioneering aviator, bears the dubious distinction of being the first English citizen ever killed in an airplane crash.

Saturn—Founded in 1985 and named after the planet, Saturn bills itself as "a new kind of car company" but is actually a division of General Motors, an old kind of car company.

Subaru—A Japanese word meaning "unite," Subaru is also the common name for the Pleiades, a cluster of six stars in the constellation of Taurus. In 1953, five Japanese companies combined to form Fuji Heavy Industries and adopted the current six-star Subaru symbol, representing FHI and its five divisions.

Toyota—Named for Sakichi Toyoda, inventor of a power loom that revolutionized the Japanese textile industry. Toyoda's company began producing automobiles in the 1930s, but when it began exporting cars after World War II the name was changed to Toyota, which was considered to have a better sound.

Jeep

It would be hard to think of a vehicle more quintessentially American—tough, perhaps a little rough, but ready for anything—than the Jeep, now manufactured by DaimlerChrysler.

The history of the Jeep brand is well known, from its origins on the battlefields of World War II, where Jeeps served as all-purpose four-wheel-drive transport vehicles, to the refined suburban SUVs of today, but the name Jeep itself has long been a subject of etymological contention.

Some theories trace Jeep to the vehicle's supposed military designation GP, standing for "general purpose." Unfortunately, the U.S. military never designated any vehicle GP. Interestingly, however, a larger truck that preceded the Jeep in light transport duty was known among soldiers as the "Peep."

The true origin of Jeep seems to lie in another bit of classic Americana—the *Popeye* comic strip. In March 1936, *Popeye* creator Elzie C. Segar introduced a strange new character in the strip, more of an animal, actually, about the size of a dog but walking upright and equipped with all sorts of mysterious powers, including telepathy and invisibility. The critter was called Eugene the Jeep, probably because the only sound it could make was a cry of "Jeep! Jeep!"

But Eugene the Jeep could do just about anything he wanted to in the *Popeye* strip, so it made sense that when soldiers encountered the new all-purpose do-anything vehicle in the Army, the successor to the Peep, they would dub it the Jeep.

Land Rover

Land Rover owners and their yuppified Range Rover–flaunting cousins may be a little chagrined to learn that the moniker of their rugged but pricey rides first graced that humblest of kiddie conveyances—the tricycle.

First produced by a bicycle firm in Coventry, England, in 1887, Rover tricycles were eventually superseded by Rover cars in 1904, and by the beginning of World War II, Rover had become one of Britain's most popular auto brands.

After the war, however, stringent government steel rationing put a crimp in Rover's production and imperiled the future of the company. A new product was needed, preferably one that used as little steel as possible. Two of Rover's directors, brothers Maurice and Spencer Wilks, decided that the market was wide open for a utility vehicle similar to the American Jeep so widely used in the war, and set out to design their own version. Using as little of the scarce steel as possible, they built the chassis out of light but strong aluminum alloy and debuted their creation in 1948, choosing the name Land Rover to convey the vehicle's rugged four-wheel-drive ability to traverse any kind of terrain. The Land Rover was an immediate success, and subsequent models were popular with both civilians and many of the world's armies.

By the late 1960s, the emergence of the recreational off-road vehicle market led to the development of a more refined version of the Land Rover, one that would combine rugged construction with the cushier comforts of Rover's standard car lines. The result, introduced in 1970, was the Range Rover, the name conjuring up visions not of explorers or soldiers, but country gentry spending Sunday afternoon inspecting their vast estates. Or maybe just looking cool driving to the local mall.

Mercedes-Benz

Mercedes-Benz automobiles, one of the world's luxury brands, are the legacy of two innovators in the motor car industry at the beginning of the twentieth century. But neither was named Mercedes.

Gottlieb Daimler and Carl Benz were born only a few miles and ten years apart in mid-nineteenth century Germany; they pursued parallel careers but did not work together until late in their lives. Both Daimler and Benz formed their own car companies in the 1880s and produced lines of automobiles under their own names until economic necessity dictated the merger of their companies in 1926 into Daimler-Benz.

While Daimler was still an independent corporation in 1898, an Austrian financier named Emil Jellinek approached the company, requesting increasingly powerful cars for use in his hobby of auto racing, particularly in the French Tour de Nice race. In entering the race with his Daimler car, Jellinek used the pseudonym Mercedes, the name of his ten-year-old daughter. Jellinek worked with Daimler for several years distributing their cars and collaborating on designs, and eventually his race pseudonym was adopted by Daimler as the model name of a race car in 1900. Conventional "Mercedes" cars followed, and the Mercedes brand became so famous all over Europe that when Daimler and Benz finally merged, the resulting primary brand was Mercedes-Benz, with Daimler-Benz relegated to secondary use.

Meanwhile, Emil Jellinek, aware of the commercial significance of his pseudonym, asked and got permission from Daimler to legally call himself Jellinek-Mercedes, noting, "This is probably the first time that a father has taken his daughter's name."

Saab

Mazda has sold a lot of cars with its catchy "zoom-zoom" jingle, but a case could be made that the motto really belongs to Saab, a car company that was zooming long before it made its first automobile.

Svenska Aeroplan Aktiebolaget was formed in 1937 as Sweden's national manufacturer of military aircraft. After World War II, company engineers realized that the expertise in design they had acquired in building combat aircraft would translate well to the building of automobiles, and launched a secret car project in 1945. In 1947, they presented their first prototype in public, a highly advanced auto design that featured front-wheel drive, a safety cage surrounding its passengers, and an aerodynamic design based on the shape of an aircraft wing. The Model 92 was a hit with the public when it was released two years later, and the world discovered the Saab brand, an acronym formed from *Svenska Aeroplan AktieBo-laget.*

More than twenty thousand Model 92s were built over the next seven years, and Saab has since become famous for its pioneering engineering, safety, and comfort. Saab also still makes aircraft, including high-performance military and commercial jets.

Volkswagen

For a car brand whose success has often been viewed as the triumph of a spunky underdog, Volkswagen's most impressive accomplishment may be overcoming just about the worst origin imaginable.

Ferdinand Porsche was a highly respected automobile designer in 1933 when he was called to a meeting with Adolf Hitler, who had recently become chancellor in Germany. Hitler had a plan to solidify his support among the German people by promising them a low-priced, durable German-made car, the automotive equivalent of "a chicken in every pot." Hitler not only laid out precise requirements for the car in his meeting with Porsche but insisted that the car be sold for under 1,000 marks (about $250 at that time). And Hitler wanted Porsche to organize and oversee the project.

Porsche had no objection to the idea of a small, mass-produced car. He had even produced two prototypes of such a vehicle several years earlier. It was the price that seemed impossible; even Henry Ford, the genius behind the mass production of cars, had never built a car he could sell for less than twice that price.

Within months, however, Porsche realized that Hitler's impractical plan was an order, not a suggestion. Hitler began giving speeches in which he promised his followers that his regime would soon make the Volkswagen (literally, "Peoples' Car") available to every German citizen. So Porsche spent the next few years developing prototypes of the Volkswagen and gearing up production at a factory in Wolfsburg. Ironically, by 1939 Hitler's appetite for war scuttled his dream of the Volkswagen. With the Nazi invasion of Czechoslovakia and Poland, production at the Wolfsburg plant was switched to military vehicles, and the first Volkswagen Beetle (of which more than 21 million were eventually sold) was not produced until after the war.

It was also after the war that Ferdinand Porsche was finally able to return to his real passion, designing racing and sports cars. Today Porsche A.G. produces upscale sports and passenger cars.

Volvo

Perhaps the most popular Swedish import to the United States (at least between the departure of Abba and the arrival of IKEA), Volvo automobiles and trucks sport a nearly ideal brand name for motor vehicles: two short alliterative syllables connoting a sense of power and motion.

Volvo is not only the best-known Swedish automobile, it

was the first, dating back to the 1920s. But the name Volvo itself is not Swedish.

Assar Gabrielsson and Gustaf Larson were both working at the time for the Swedish company SKF, producing and marketing ball bearings. In 1924, Gabrielsson and Larson, who had worked in England as an engine designer, formed a partnership to design and build cars, producing their first model in 1925. SKF soon took an interest, providing factory space and financing. When the time came to pick a name for the new venture, SKF gave the partners permission to call their company AB Volvo. The name had been used previously by SKF for the ball-bearing subsidiary where the two men worked, and was chosen because Volvo, derived from the Latin for "I roll," was considered as appropriate for cars as for ball bearings.

The Volvo symbol, an arrow emerging from a circle, is thought by many to be based on the astrological symbol for Mars (commonly considered the symbol for male) but is actually a modification of an ancient alchemist's symbol for iron ore.

DRUGS AND COSMETICS

Ivory Soap

Harley Procter didn't need any fancy-schmancy naming consultants to pick a moniker for his company's new soap. He had divine inspiration.

Back in 1878, Procter's partner, James Norris Gamble, had just developed a distinctive white soap, and their firm of Procter & Gamble, which had been making soap and candles in Cincinnati, Ohio, since 1837, was planning to market it as P&G White Soap. But Harley Procter wasn't satisfied with the drab name and spent several weeks mulling over possible alternatives. But nothing really clicked, and it looked as if P&G White Soap was headed for the market burdened with its boring name.

But one Sunday morning, the minister in Procter's church chose for his sermon Psalm 45, which includes the line "All thy garments smell of myrrh, and aloes, and cassia, out of the ivory palaces, whereby they have made thee glad."

Garments . . . Fragrances . . . Palaces . . . Bingo! Procter had the perfect name for his new soap, and the first bars of Ivory soap hit the market in 1879.

Oddly enough, two of Ivory's best marketing slogans were later developments, and perhaps the most popular feature of Ivory Soap was entirely accidental. Early on, P&G submitted samples of Ivory soap to various laboratories for analysis, and one lab reported that the soap showed only .56 percent non-soap ingredients. Harley Procter did some simple subtraction, and Ivory's trademarked slogan "99–44/100% Pure" was born.

During the same period, a worker in the P&G factory failed to turn off the soap-mixing machine when he went to lunch one day, and returned to find the product in a slightly frothy condition. But since the soap seemed to be fine aside from the bubbles, it was molded and shipped as usual. Only weeks later when the P&G marketing department reported receiving strange orders for "the floating soap" did the company realize that the worker's inattention had whipped enough air into the soap that it actually floated on water. Ever since, P&G has deliberately mixed small amounts of air into Ivory, and "It Floats" joined Ivory's "99–44/100% Pure" slogan in 1891.

Listerine

Sir Joseph Lister, pioneer germ fighter and proselytizer for sterile operating rooms, did not invent Listerine, but his career inspired it.

In 1876, a pharmacist named Joseph Lawrence saw Lister demonstrate his sterilization techniques using carbolic acid and was inspired to join the antiseptic fight.

Lister's initial method of sterilizing operating theaters was to fill the room with carbolic acid mist, which did kill the germs that caused infection but was a bit hard on the surgeons. Many were eventually forced to cease operating because over time the acid bleached their skin and made breathing painful.

Understandably, Lawrence felt that carbolic acid was too strong for normal use. In 1879, he developed his own milder formula, which he dubbed Listerine to honor Lister.

Lawrence's invention was a disinfectant, not a mouthwash, and at first it was sold only to physicians. It was businessman Jordan Lambert who bought the rights to Listerine from Lawrence in 1884 and turned it into today's Listerine mouthwash.

Mary Kay

"I couldn't believe God meant a woman's brain to bring 50 cents on the dollar," Mary Kay Ash once said, and she spent the second half of her life proving that she knew more about earning dollars than most men.

She had been born into poverty in Hot Wells, Texas, and supported herself and her children after World War II working for Stanley Home Products, organizing Tupperware-style home sales parties. Mary Kay proved so good at sales that she became the national training director for another direct sales company, but she eventually quit, frustrated that the men she trained were always promoted to positions above her.

In 1963, while developing an outline for the book on sales she was planning to write, Mary Kay realized that she could and should start her own company instead of just writing about it. Starting with just eleven sales reps selling her line of cosmetics in distinctive pink packaging direct to consumers, Mary Kay Ash built Mary Kay, Inc. into a global empire with annual revenues of $1.3 billion. Mary Kay died in November 2001, at age eighty-six.

Oddly enough, Mary Kay is probably best known for something she never sold: cars. She bought her first Cadillac in 1968 and had the dealer repaint it her favorite color, pink. Recognizing the stir the car caused, she turned it into a motivational prize for her sales force, awarding a pink Cadillac sedan to any employee who achieved sales of $15,000 per month for six consecutive months.

Noxzema

It was pretty clear from Day One that Dr. George Bunting was going to have to find a better name for his product. Even by the standards of 1914, when Bunting introduced his new cosmetic cream, the name he had chosen, Doctor Bunting's Sunburn Remedy, was not going to perch easily on the nation's lips.

Fortunately, his first customers loved Dr. Bunting's greaseless cream with its aroma of camphor, menthol, and eucalyptus instead of the greasy, tallow-based concoctions then on the market. And one customer even solved the name problem with his fan mail. Doctor Bunting's Sunburn Remedy, he declared, had "knocked" the eczema that had been torturing him. Knocked eczema? Noxzema was born.

Olay

So what's in that "mysterious beauty fluid" advertised as Oil of Olay? And what's an olay, anyway? A plant? A place? A small mammal? The cry of a bullfighter who spies wrinkles in the mirror?

None of the above, as far as anyone can tell. As a matter of fact, it seems that there is no such thing as an "olay," and that the name was just a clever marketing ploy by its inventors, especially since the mysterious moisturizer wasn't even called Oil of Olay at first.

Oil of Olay was developed during World War II by a South African chemist named Graham Gordon Wulff to help military burn victims heal by preventing their skin from becoming dehydrated. Whether the original ingredients (glycerin, various vegetable oils, etc.) remain in Olay today is a trade secret, but at the end of the war it occurred to Wulff that the burn treatment he had invented might make a dandy beauty cream in the civilian market. He teamed up with a partner named Shaun Adams Lowe, and together they set out to market Wulff's cream.

First, of course, they needed a name, and after some thought came up with Oil of Ulay. Ulay, not Olay. At first the two sold their cream door to door in South Africa. As more people bought it and asked what "Ulay" was, Wulff and Lowe realized that the mystery of their product's name was one of its strongest selling points, and "the mysterious beauty fluid" cachet was born.

As Oil of Ulay sales caught on and the product was exported to Europe and the United States, a curious adjustment of its name took place. In England it was still called Oil of Ulay, but in most of Europe it was sold under the name Oil of Olaz. Only in America was it called Oil of Olay. There does not appear to have been any particular reason for the different names, but it wasn't until 2000 that Ulay/Olay/Olaz owners Procter & Gamble decided to simplify life by changing it to Olay worldwide. Today Olay (they dropped the "Oil of" a few years ago) produces a wide range of beauty products.

Prozac

Prozac is, in addition to being the most famous prescription drug on the planet at the moment, an excellent example of the new method of naming pharmaceutical products. There was a time when a physician prescribing an antidepressant for a patient would simply have scrawled the drug's technical name—in the case of Prozac, the tongue-twisting fluoxetine—on a prescription pad. In the unlikely event that the patient could actually read the name, it would probably be meaningless to him.

But that was before drugs became consumer products, advertised (ad nauseam, many would say) directly to prospective patients on television and in glossy magazine ads. To catch the eyes of customers, rather than those of their doctors, pharmaceutical companies in the early 1990s began to name their drugs using the same linguistic principles used to name cars, beers, and laundry detergents. The new generation of drug names thus has absolutely nothing to do with the clinical properties of the drug itself and everything to do with the patient's expectation of a quick and effective solution to a problem.

In the case of Prozac, the connotation is powerful action (from the strong *pro-* beginning, invoking a "positive" image) coupled with speed (the *z* sound) and ending with the solid, powerful "ac" suggesting "action" and providing a firm, punchy ending to the name. If Prozac weren't a drug, it would be a good name for a gasoline.

Q-Tips

It wasn't exactly Archimedes and his eureka moment (see page 116), but Leo Gerstenzang also found his best idea in a bathtub.

In Leo's case, it was by watching his wife giving their baby a bath one day in 1923. To clean the baby's ears, he noticed, Mrs. Gerstenzang twisted cotton balls around the ends of toothpicks. This struck Leo, who just happened to own the Leo Gerstenzang Infant Novelty Co. in New York City, as a clever (if cumbersome and potentially dangerous) technique, and he decided to spend some time refining her invention.

Leo did spend quite a bit of time developing his little sticks, making sure the wood wouldn't splinter and the cotton wouldn't fall off (and lodge in baby's ear), but finally he was satisfied and ready to market his swabs through his baby-care shop.

But first he needed a name for his new invention, and after some thought, he came up with one.

One really odd, awful name, that is. He called them Baby Gays.

Baby Gays sold well, but someone must have clued Leo into just how weird the name was, because within a couple of years he had changed it to Q-tips Baby Gays, and finally simply to Q-tips. The *Q* is said to stand for quality. Today Q-tips are churned out at the rate of 25.5 billion per year but are not recommended by most pediatricians for use in babies' (or anyone else's) ears.

Vaseline

There are two different stories, one a bit goofy, the other perhaps a little too dignified, about the origin of the name Vaseline, the trade name of the petroleum jelly invented by Robert A. Chesebrough in 1870.

The goofy story is that Chesebrough, looking around for containers in which to store his invention, swiped a few of his wife's flower vases. Once he decided that the time had come to name his new goo, he simply combined *vase* with the then-popular chemical suffix *-line.*

The more somber we-are-serious-scientists version eschews flower vases and credits Chesebrough with combining *Wasser,* the German word for water, with *elaion,* Greek for "oil."

If this account is true, Chesebrough deserves even more

credit for mixing the German and Greek and coming up with Vaseline, rather than Wasserelaion, which would have been a sure ticket to oblivion.

So take your pick of the two stories, but don't use Vaseline as a generic term for petroleum jelly. It's still a trademark of Unilever.

Viagra

The easiest way to explain how to pronounce Viagra, Pfizer's flagship anti-impotence drug, is simply to note that it rhymes with Niagara, as in Niagara Falls, the archetypal honeymoon locale that conjures up fantasies of love and romance (and, of course, energetic sex) in the minds of most Americans.

The association between Viagra and Niagara is hardly a co-incidence, but even that powerful hook needed a little semantic tweaking. The initial "vi" syllable combines *v*, a highly energetic consonant, with intimations of vitality and vigor, while "agra" skirts just close enough to "aggression" to connote force and power. Put it all together and you have a word with no intrinsic meaning but which suggests a fountain of sexual youth.

Bibliography

Most of the information in this book regarding the origin of particular brand names was gathered from the manufacturers themselves, either through direct correspondence with their public relations departments (for whose enthusiastic cooperation I am very grateful) or from their corporate Web sites, many of which helpfully post detailed accounts of the history of their brands.

Additional details about many brands, as well as information about the history and practice of branding and marketing, were gathered from a wide variety of newspapers, magazines, and industry publications accessed through the electronic databases of the Columbus Metropolitan Library of Columbus, Ohio, and the New York Public Library in New York City.

The following books were also very helpful, and may be of interest for further reading:

Campbell, Hannah. *Why Did They Name It . . . ?* New York: Fleet Press Corporation, 1964.

Dibbley, Dale Corey. *From Achilles' Heel to Zeus's Shield.* New York: Fawcett Columbine, 1993.

Dickson, Paul. *What's in a Name?: Reflections of an Irrepressible Name Collector.* Springfield, Mass.: Merriam-Webster, 1996.

Kearney, Mark, and Randy Ray. *I Know That Name!: The People Behind Canada's Best-Known Brand Names From Elizabeth Arden to Walter Zeller.* Toronto: Dundurn Press, 2002.

Lass, Abraham H., David Kiremidjian, and Ruth M. Goldstein. *The Facts on File Dictionary of Classical, Biblical and Literary Allusions.* New York: Facts on File Publications, 1987.

Lee, Laura. *The Name's Familiar: Mr. Leotard, Barbie and Chef Boyardee.* Gretna, La.: Pelican Publishing Company, 1999.

Room, Adrian. *Trade Name Origins.* New York: McGraw Hill, 1996.

Acknowledgments

Thanks to my wife, Kathy Wollard, for suggesting many of the brand names in this book, as well as for her always invaluable advice and support; to my agent, Janis Donnaud, for her hard work and advice; to Amanda Patten and everyone at Simon & Schuster for shepherding this book into print, and to eagle-eyed copy editor Sybil Pincus, for catching my flubs and clarifying my prose.